Date Loaned			
	6-25-82		

Library Bureau Cat. No. 1138

BARUCH SPINOZA
AND WESTERN DEMOCRACY

ALSO BY JOSEPH DUNNER:

Published in Switzerland:
DIE GEWERKSCHAFTEN IM ARBEITSKAMPF

Published in the United States:
IF I FORGET THEE . . .
THE REPUBLIC OF ISRAEL, ITS HISTORY AND ITS PROMISE
DEMOCRATIC BULWARK IN THE MIDDLE EAST

Co-author of:
MAJOR ASPECTS OF INTERNATIONAL POLITICS
AMERICAN EXPERIENCES IN MILITARY GOVERNMENT IN
   WORLD WAR II
INTERNATIONALISM AND DEMOCRACY
CONSTITUTIONS AND CONSTITUTIONAL TRENDS SINCE
   WORLD WAR II

BARUCH SPINOZA
AND
WESTERN DEMOCRACY

AN INTERPRETATION OF HIS PHILOSOPHICAL,
RELIGIOUS AND POLITICAL THOUGHT

by
JOSEPH DUNNER
Professor of Political Science at Grinnell College

PHILOSOPHICAL LIBRARY
NEW YORK

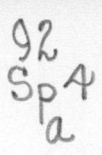

Copyright, 1955, by the Philosophical Library, Inc.,
15 East 40th Street, New York, 16, N. Y.

All rights reserved.

Printed in the United States of America
By The Haddon Craftsmen, Inc.

*This book is dedicated to
three faithful friends:*
HAROLD A. GOLDMAN
RAPHAEL MALSIN
and
PAUL UHLMANN

Under the conditions of the time and in the place the ban [against Spinoza] was perhaps justified . . . but as the condemnation of Socrates by an Athenian court did not turn that great Greek philosopher into a non-Greek, so the rabbinical ban in Amsterdam in the seventeenth century cannot deprive the Jewish people of its greatest and most original thinker.

DAVID BEN-GURION

[*From a letter to the author dated October 4, 1954*]

O Lord, my life was known to Thee
Ere Thou hadst caused me yet to be,
Thy Spirit ever dwells in me.
    JEHUDA HALEVI
    (1086-1145 A.D.)

Deum rerum omnium causam immanentem . . .
          SPINOZA

CONTENTS

Acknowledgments   xiii

Spinoza's Life   1

    THE "GOLDEN AGE" OF HISPANO-JEWISH CULTURE   2
    THE MARRANOS   4
    URIEL ACOSTA   7
    SPINOZA LEAVES THE JODENBURT   10
    TRACTATUS BREVIS   13
    SPINOZA REFUSES TO ACCEPT HEIDELBERG PROFESSORSHIP   21
    A "GODLESS" TREATISE   26
    DEATH AT THE AGE OF 44   34

Spinoza's Metaphysics   35

    SUBSTANCE, CAUSE AND ATTRIBUTE   37
    DESCARTES' DUALISM   38
    DEUS SIVE NATURA   40
    ON HUMAN FREEDOM   51
    MI AFAR ATA . . .   54
    FROM METAPHYSICS TO POLITICS   55

Spinoza's Concept of God   58

    MAIMONIDES AND THOMAS AQUINAS   58
    OF PROPHECY   59
    ETHICAL AND METAPHYSICAL ATTRIBUTES OF GOD   62
    MIRACLES   70
    NATURA NATURATA   72
    THE CHOSEN PEOPLE   74

RELIGION AND CIVILIZATION	79
UNIVERSAL FAITH	82
JESUS, THE LAST JEWISH PROPHET OF OLD	85

Spinoza's Political Thought — 89

THE DUTCH REVOLT	89
SPINOZA ESSENTIALLY A POLITICAL SCIENTIST	90
HOBBES' *Leviathan* AND SPINOZA'S CONCEPT OF THE STATE	91
FREEDOM OF THOUGHT AND SPEECH	106
SELF-PRESERVATION, NOT SELF-INDULGENCE	113
SPINOZA, PATH FINDER OF MODERN DEMOCRACY	119

Spinoza's Legacy for the Twentieth Century — 122

WHAT IS ATHEISM?	123
A TASK FOR COLLEGES AND CHURCHES	123
COMPLETENESS OF PERSONALITY	125
THE COMMUNIST CHALLENGE	132
DEMOCRACY AND ETHICS	138

Acknowledgments

I wish to acknowledge my obligation to the University Library of Amsterdam for the use of the original copy of Johann Colero's biography of Spinoza and to Dover Publications, Inc. for the use of the 1951 edition of *The Chief Works of Benedict De Spinoza*, translated from the Latin, with an introduction by R. H. M. Elwes. Most of my quotations of Spinoza's writings have been taken from this one-volume edition. I am indebted to the Jewish Reconstructionist Movement, particularly the books and articles written by Professor Mordecai Kaplan, for many new insights which have helped me in my approach to Spinozistic concepts. I am grateful to Dr. C. Edwin Gilmour, my colleague in the Department of Political Science at Grinnell, for reading my manuscript and to Dr. Paul Kuntz of the Grinnell Department of Religion and Philosophy for having given me various valuable suggestions. Finally, I want to thank my wife for her encouragement in all my writings. I remain responsible for such errors of fact and interpretation as the book contains.

The manuscript was completed on July 27, 1954, in Amsterdam, Holland.

JOSEPH DUNNER

Spinoza's Life

BARUCH SPINOZA was born on November 24, 1632 in Amsterdam, where his parents, Spanish-Portuguese Jews, had sought refuge from the Inquisition in the Iberian peninsula. Though not much is known of Michael and Hana Debora Spinoza, we have it on the authority of Johann Colero,[1] a Lutheran pastor at The Hague and Spinoza's first biographer, as well as in the writings of Berthold Auerbach,[2] the German-Jewish novelist, that Baruch's parents, like so many Jewish parents, saved every penny and sacrificed even normal comforts of life in order to give their son the most thorough Jewish and general education according to the standards of their time.

The Spinozas (or Despinozas) came from a country in which the Jews had risen to unparalleled power and achievement. A thousand years after the destruction of the second Jewish commonwealth by the legions of Rome, sub-

---

[1] Das Leben des Bened. von Spinoza, aus denen Schrifften Dieses beruffenen Welt-Weisens und aus dem Zeugniss vieler glaubwürdigen Personen, die ihn besonders gekannt haben, gezogen und beschrieben von Johann Colero, Ehemaligen Prediger der Evangelischen Gemeinde in Haag; Nunmehro aber aus dem Frantzösischen ins Hoch-Teutsche übersetzt und mit verschiedenen Ammerkungen vermehrt. Frankfurt und Leipzig MDCCXXXIII. In a footnote (page 7) of his biography, Johann Colero writes: "The late Christian Korthold, in his book *De Tribus Impostoribus Magnis,* has remarked: 'His name is Benedict von Spinoza whom, however, one should call a Maledict, for our thorny earth, cursed by God, has produced no human being as cursed as he was and no writings so full of thorns as his.'" (My translation).

[2] B. de Spinoza's Sämmtliche Werke aus Dem Lateinischen mit einer Lebensgeschichte Spinoza's von Berthold Auerbach, Stuttgart 1871, Verlag der J. G. Cotta'schen Buchhandlung, 2 Bände.

jected to civil discrimination and inferiority in most of the diaspora (dispersion), branded by a mighty state-church as the people rejected by God for the crucifixion of "the Savior",[3] exposed to the fanaticism of priests, crusaders and an ever-credulous populace, the Jews of Spain and Portugal, under the beneficent sway of Islam, had been able to refashion their civilization and, though few in numbers, to surpass in intellectual eminence all the young and vigorous nations of Europe. "While those around them were grovelling in the darkness of besotted ignorance, while juggling miracles and lying relics were the themes on which almost all Europe was expatiating, while the intellect of Christendom, enthralled by countless superstitions, had sunk into a deadly torpor . . . the Jews were still pursuing the path of knowledge, amassing learning and stimulating progress with the same unflinching constancy that they had manifested in their faith. They were the most skilful physicians, the ablest financiers, and among the most profound philosophers . . ."[4]

This, of course, is not the place to review the historical record of the "Golden Age" of Hispano-Jewish culture. But a few data, necessary for an understanding of Baruch Spinoza's very topics of discussion, must be mentioned.

Hebrew poetry which had been dormant since the days of the Maccabees had been revived under the influence of the happy days experienced by the Jews of Spain and Portugal. Solomon ibn Gabirol (1021-58) whose best known poem "Kether Malchuth" (The Crown of Kingdom) has been incorporated into the liturgy for the eve of the Day

[3] At the time of Jesus, the power to inflict death in Roman occupied Judea was a Roman privilege. In Matthew, Pilate, the Roman governor, asks what he shall do to "Jesus which is called the Christ." It would be the only instance that Pilate ever asked the enslaved Jews for guidance. The whole account appears to be unhistorical and written to please the rulers of the Roman empire.

[4] W. E. H. Leeky, *History of Rationalism*, p. 282.

of Atonement, and Jehuda Halevi (1086-1140) whose songs of Zion inspired many Jewish generations, were inspirations to Baruch Spinoza in his youth. A subject of deep concern to the medieval Jew was the interpretation of the Scriptures, and in this field two Spanish Jews played the most prominent part. One of them, Abraham ibn Ezra (1092-1167) may well be called the first rationalist critic of the Bible; and it is to him, who wrote his commentary on Holy Writ when even the original text was virtually unknown to the ecclesiastics of Europe, that Baruch Spinoza turned as soon as he felt the orthodoxy of the Amsterdam Jewish community too fettering. The other, one of the giants of the Jewish people, was Moses ben Maimon, called Maimonides (1135-1205). A physician by profession, for some time court physician of Sultan Saladin of Egypt, Maimonides wrote on mathematics, astronomy—astrology he declared unworthy of attention—the Bible and the Talmud.[5] Steeped in the writings of Plato, Aristotle, and the Alexandrian Jewish philosopher Philo, Maimonides, in his attempt to graft Greek rationalism on the theological symbolism of the Old Testament, preceded by close to a hundred years the great champion of the papal cause, Thomas Aquinas. Yet, while Judaism up to Maimonides' time allowed the widest philosophical speculation, so long as the Ten Commandments were respected, it was Maimonides, who in *Yad Hasakah* (Mighty Hand) and *Moreh Nebuchim* (A Guide of the Perplexed), inaugurated a hitherto unknown dogmatism which in thirteen fundamental principles of faith has remained the accepted basis of orthodox Judaism. It was this dogmatic concept of

---

[5] The Talmud is a rabbinically authorized commentary largely concerned with the legal points of the Bible and with customs of Jewish communal life.

Judaism, not Judaism as a way of life and a dynamic civilization, that Baruch Spinoza came to reject.

The Sephardim,[6] as the Jews of Spain and Portugal are called, unlike their coreligionists in other parts of Europe, were not degraded strangers in a strange land, but Spaniards in speech and thought, combining the graces of a high civilization and the chivalry of the Spanish gentleman with an enlightened faith. While the Jews of England, France, Germany and Italy lived in servitude, distinguished even in their garb by a hideous "badge of shame" which the Lateran Church Council of 1215 had compelled the Jews to wear, the Jews of Spain were the ministers of the State, the diplomats, the highest dignitaries of the realm.

The more painful for them, then, was the onslaught of the Church which, having enforced its supremacy over the rest of Europe, at last turned to destroy the hateful competition of Judaism in Spain. Fiercely inveighing against Jewish "unbelief", inciting an ignorant and exploited mass of people to murder and plunder the more prosperous Jews, the friars and other agents of the Spanish Church attacked the Jewish communities in one city after another. Not a few Jews, setting their trust in the promises of Pope Benedict XIII to protect converts, accepted baptism in the hope of escaping the horrors which the Spanish-Catholic priesthood inflicted on the unconverted Jews. But the ecclesiastical authorities suspected, not without justification, that while outwardly Christians, most of the converted Jews retained their Jewish beliefs and practices. The Inquisition, together with the Nazi and Soviet torture cells, the vilest institution ever devised to enslave the human spirit, was, therefore, unleashed on the Marranos (the Jewish Christians), who by accepting the shelter of the Church had robbed the former Christians of the right to

---

[6] Sepharad is the traditional Hebrew name of Spain.

burn them at stake in a festive auto-da-fé (act of faith) and to steal their earthly belongings. Infuriated by the perseverance of the Jews and Marranos, the Church finally, in 1492, resolved to expel all the 300,000 Jews of Spain, many converts to Catholicism among them.[7]

Those who, afraid of the long journey to Islamic Turkey or Protestant Holland, went to neighboring Portugal were immediately coerced into baptism or sold as slaves. While the Marranos of Portugal carried on their secret practices of Judaism for centuries afterward, numbers of them continually migrated to other parts of Europe where they could openly profess their ancestral faith. Michael and Hana Debora Despinoza were such Marranos who in the beginning of the 17th century had escaped from Portugal to live as free citizens and Jews in hospitable Amsterdam.[8]

Thanks to his home environment, Baruch was raised in three tongues; Spanish, Portuguese and Hebrew. Dutch, as we learn from his recently discovered letters, he spoke and wrote with difficulty. At the Jewish High School, known as a Heder (room), he studied the Five Books of Moses and the Talmud, first under Morteira, a well known Talmudist, and later under Rabbi Manasseh ben Israel, who in 1655 was employed by the Jews of Western Europe to petition from Oliver Cromwell the readmission of the Jews to England. It was Manasseh ben Israel, himself the son of a Marrano family from Lisbon, who introduced Baruch to the Cabbalah.

[7] Strangely enough, the day of the deportation of the Jews in Spain was the day on which Columbus (according to Salvador de Madariaga), probably himself a Marrano, sailed on his voyage which led to the discovery of the American Continent.
[8] In 1579 the representatives of the northern provinces of the Netherlands had assembled in Utrecht to declare that their country, liberated from the Spaniards, should be an asylum of religious tolerance. Every citizen "should be accorded freedom of worship and no one should be molested on account of his belief."

Cabbalah (which literally means tradition) had its origin in the esoteric speculations of the Essenes, a Jewish sect of which John the Baptist and probably also Jesus of Nazareth were initiated members. The work of creation, related in Genesis, was the great and continuous theme that preoccupied the Cabbalists and caused them to concoct a medley of Jewish religious thought, Greek philosophy, and all sorts of magic notions which under the form of Gnosticism produced a rather serious menace to the orthodox development of Christianity. In the most important literary product of Cabbalah, the Zohar (Splendor), attributed to the authorship of the famous Rabbi Simon ben Johai (in the second century A.D.), God was conceived as En Soph, the Infinite, with ten Sephiroth or "Emanations" which were to describe the essence of the Deity and to resolve the riddle of life. These "Emanations" were to play a significant role in Spinoza's concept of God.

The darker the physical world grew for the Jews of the diaspora and the more widespread pogroms and other persecutions became, the more they took refuge in Talmudic hair splitting and cabbalistic mysticism, the more their innate optimism turned into a gloomy asceticism which looked upon the earthly world as a vale of tears. Typical for the time and expressive of Jewish hopes for the return to the security of a national home were the pseudo-Messiahs, chief among them David Reubeni, who posed as the ambassador of a Jewish king of Chaibar in the Arabian peninsula and Sabbatai Zevi, a Turkish Jew. Both were convinced that they had the magic formula to free the Holy Land from the hands of the Gentiles and to usher in the Messianic era for the Jewish people, and both failed miserably.

If we are to accept Berthold Auerbach's account, it was

Rabbi Manasseh ben Israel, Rembrandt's friend,[9] who once told Baruch Spinoza that Jesus, the rabbi of Nazareth in Galilee, had been a Cabbalist. Whether by coincidence or not, shortly afterward Baruch began to read the New Testament, known to most Jews only by hearsay and considered by the orthodox as the work of Satan.

There was little sympathy in the Jodenburt, the Jewish quarter of Amsterdam, with anything that smacked of skepticism and reform. Unlike the Ashkenazim[10] (German Jews), the Sephardic colony was made up to a large extent of reverts from Catholicism, and the virus of the papal Church was still with them. It revealed itself in the Gregorian chant used when intoning prayers, in the insistence on minute detail in ritual, and in the most rigid orthodoxy. There was no Sephardic Jew in Amsterdam who did not have a personal memory of the torments which members of his family had to endure in Spain and Portugal; and all former Marranos had some experience with inquisitorial dungeons and tortures accompanied by an Ave Maria gratia plena. These Jews had found out that whoever was not with them was against them; and they tolerated no heresies in their midst. Moreover, they wanted to make sure that the non-Jews of Holland would never be able to accuse them of atheism, the worst crime of the age.

Baruch was but eight years old when Uriel Acosta had been buried. Acosta, a Portuguese Marrano, reared as a Catholic, had fled to Amsterdam in the hope of finding there among his fellow Jews the freedom of thought and expression which had characterized Jewish life in the "Golden Age" of Spain. When he discovered that the lofty moral

---

[9] Many of Rembrandt's portraits of Jewish men actually show the features of Manasseh ben Israel.
[10] Ashkenaz is the traditional Hebrew word for the Germanic territories.

values of prophetic Judaism had been drowned in a sea of medieval scholasticism and authoritarianism, affecting Christians and Jews alike, he wrote a vituperative book against the rabbis, accusing them of being "Pharisees." Actually the Pharisees of ancient Israel, in contrast to the Sadducean priest caste, had represented the more liberal tradition of Judaism recognizing the principle of religious evolution. Rabbi Hillel was a Pharisee. His famous words, "Do not unto others what you would not have others do unto you; this is the law, all else is commentary," can certainly not be interpreted as legalism and religious reaction. Joseph of Arimathea, whom Matthew describes as a disciple of Jesus and whom Luke calls "a good man and just", identified himself as a Pharisee. The term "Pharisee" in its negative connotation Acosta had learned from his Jesuit teachers in Portugal, who in the tradition of the Greek church fathers, many of them former pagans, did not know and understand the Jewish tradition. If any comparison can be made, the Sephardic rabbis of Amsterdam behaved like Spanish priests in handling Acosta. They lodged a complaint against him before the Amsterdam magistrates, caused his brochure to be prohibited, and excommunicated him from their synagogue.

After fifteen years of isolation from the Jewish community, Acosta recanted; but soon again he was at odds with his fellow Jews. Again, he was put in the rabbinical ban; and again he recanted and promised to live as an observing Jew. The last time the Amsterdam Sephardic congregation drew up a penance modelled on what its members had seen used in the Catholic churches of Spain and Portugal. The wretched man was forced to read before the assembled congregation a confession of his sins. They were: desecration of the Sabbath, violation of the dietary laws, and derision of the faith. Then he was made to bend his back to receive thirty-nine lashes with a whip, all of them to the accompaniment of verses from the Psalms. Only then was the excommunication revoked. The same day Acosta loaded two pistols. With one he fired on a fellow Jew who passed by his home and missed. The other he turned on himself. This time he did not miss.

It is quite possible that Michael Despinoza reminded his son of Acosta's fate when Baruch, at the age of eighteen, asked for permission to study Latin, the language of the Catholic church. Realizing, however, that Latin was the passport to much of the knowledge of the time, he secured a Latin teacher for Baruch. The name of this teacher was Van den Ende. He was a Catholic by birth; and though he considered himself an agnostic, he was nevertheless suspected by the good Calvinistic burghers of Amsterdam as an agent of Rome. It was through Van den Ende that Spinoza familiarized himself with the natural sciences. The Old Testament vision of God, in whose glory the external world tends to disappear, had a most limited conception of nature. Scientific studies were, therefore, neglected in the Heder. Van den Ende opened a new world for Baruch, the world of Copernicus, Galileo, Kepler, Harvey, Huyghens and, last but not least, of Descartes.

According to Colero, Van den Ende had a daughter, Clara Maria, who substituted for her father whenever he, a physician by profession, was called out of the home. The pious Colero, who disliked Baruch Spinoza because of the Spinozistic principles "in point of religion", is responsible for the gossip, thoughtlessly echoed by other writers that Baruch "having often occasion to see and speak" to Clara Maria, fell in love with her. "She was none of the most beautiful, but she had a great deal of wit, a great capacity and a jovial humor which wrought upon the heart of Spinoza, as well as upon another scholar whose name was

Kerkering, a native of Hamburg . . ." To make the story short, the young lady is supposed to have displayed her sagacity by rejecting the poor Spinoza for the sake of his fellow-pupil in the Latin course, Kerkering, who allegedly was able to enhance his value by the gift of a costly pearl necklace. Actually, Van den Ende's daughter was only seven years old when Spinoza left her father's house and sixteen when he moved out of the Amsterdam region. While he never concealed his unorthodox views on religion, his whole life shows that he would have respected the wishes of his parents too much to enter intermarriage, the last thing Jewish parents, even those who have drifted from traditional Jewish life, like to see.

Michael, who had lost his first wife Hester and two of her children, had also lost Hana Debora, Baruch's and Miriam's mother, as well as his third wife, Esther. Less than a year and a half after he, Baruch, Miriam and Rebeka, a daughter of his first marriage, recited the Kaddish, the Jewish mourner's prayer, for Esther, in March 1654, he too, was carried to the grave. Baruch was twenty-two years of age when his closest bond with the Jodenburt was gone. As a son of the people of Israel, he said the Kaddish for his father for eleven months, day after day; and on the Sabbath of Hanukah, the Feast of Lights of the Jewish year 5415 or December 5, 1655, according to the Christian calendar, as the record of the Congregation Beth Jaakov (House of Jacob) shows, he was called to the altar to read from the Torah, a special honor in the Jewish ritual and certain proof that the synagogue elders still regarded him with favor.

But the time was soon to come when they were compelled to change their opinion. One day, the news reached them that Baruch Spinoza had left the Jodenburt in order to live with Van den Ende. From the fragmentary details reported by Colero, it may be deducted that Spinoza hoped to repay his host for room and board by becoming a sort of assistant instructor in Latin. He was entitled to some of the inheritance left by his father. But Rebeka, his half-sister, who, incidentally, is the first known person who called Baruch a "renegade" in order to contest his claim to their father's money and possessions, refused to part with the small family fortune. Aroused in his sense of justice, Baruch went to the "Masters of the Orphanages", a court dealing with inheritances. The court decided that next to Miriam, who had received her share in the form of the customary dowry, Baruch was the sole heir of Hana Debora's capital which Michael had sunk into his business. Since Rebeka had already appropriated most of Michael's furniture and household-goods, the court made Baruch the sole heir of the rest of the legacy. Now Rebeka went to the rabbis pleading that her "renegade" brother should not be allowed to enjoy any of the possessions of their father.

Conscious of how precarious the Jewish position was in those days, even in free Amsterdam, and afraid of a repetition of the Acosta scandal, the Jewish authorities tried to mediate between the two. Since it was seemingly money which Baruch needed for his scholarly pursuits, they offered him a yearly pension of 1,000 florins if he would leave Van den Ende and stay in their communion. Baruch, who never was interested in money, rejected their overture. Years later, in *The Ethics,* he wrote that "the free man who lives among the ignorant, strives, as far as he can, to avoid receiving favors from them."[11]

The rabbis knew, and not only from his greedy half-sister, that Baruch had come to doubt the binding force

[11] The Chief Works of Benedict de Spinoza, Translated from the Latin, with an introduction by R. H. M. Elwes, Volumes I and II bound as one. Dover Publications, Inc. New York 1951. Vol. II, p. 234.

of the Scriptures for his generation. At first, just to awaken him to his "senses", they put him in the Niddui, the "short ban", prohibiting his visits to the synagogue for a month and forbidding other Jews to keep him company during that period. It was only when Baruch, who had already moved out of the Jewish quarters and who was no longer interested in the daily worship in Beth Jaakov, did not react to their admonition to repent, that they finally pronounced the Herem, the "great ban", excommunicating him for the "horrible heresies which he practiced and taught." The writ of excommunication, dated the sixth of Ab, 5416 (July 27, 1656), written in Spanish, is still to be found in the synagogue archives. It ends with the words:

"And the Lord will separate thee from all the tribes of Israel with all the curses of the firmament which are written in the Book of the Law . . . We command that none should communicate with him orally or in writing, or show him any favor, or stay with him under the same roof, or within four ells of him, nor read anything composed or written by him."[12]

Having won the law suit against Rebeka, Baruch, though he had no funds of his own, spurned the whole inheritance. He took but "a good bed" and the necessary linen and blankets and settled in a suburb of Amsterdam, on the Ouwerkerk Road. In accordance with the time-honored Jewish custom that even the most learned rabbi should know and practice a manual trade, he had learned the art of polishing optical glasses. Lens-grinding served him now as a means for earning a living. Separated from his kindred,

[12] After the establishment of the state of Israel in 1948, pressed by Israeli newspapers, particularly "Dawar," for a revocation of the ban, the Board of the Portuguese synagogue left the ultimate decision with its chief Rabbi Salomon Rodigues Pereira. He announced his decision in these words: "No rabbinate has the right to review a decision of previous rabbinates unless it is greater in number and wiser. I don't consider myself wiser than those who came before me."

he substituted for his Hebrew name Baruch (the blessed) the Latin equivalent Benedict. But he never accepted baptism nor did he ever join any Christian congregation. He had little sympathy with the fanaticism of many of his fellow-Jews but even less with the curious superstitions of most of the Roman Catholics and Protestants of his time. Living for knowledge, he needed quiet and rest for the ordering of his thoughts.

There are sensitive persons who are too easily bruised by the often rather rough contacts with their fellow men and who, therefore, like to return to "nature". In their solitariness, they usually end up in a distrust, if not a hatred, of humanity and human ways. Spinoza was not one of them. He was rather like the prophets and apostles of Judeo-Christianity who, in their solitude and withdrawn communion with God, received the insights and the strength which caused them to return to the market places and to denounce the hypocrisies and false moral standards of their time without regard of person, however mighty and exalted. Never did Spinoza indulge in the melancholy misanthropy that distorted the philosophies of Nietzsche or Rousseau. Modern history shows no man so much above petty quibbling, so ready to forgive even his persecutors as Spinoza. No man who suffered so much injustice in his own person has made so few complaints. No man ever tried so hard to understand his fellow men and was so willing to meet them with sincere affection. As Goethe once said, "No one can produce anything important unless he isolates himself;" and Spinoza was destined to create something important. In the peaceful suburb of Amsterdam he wrote his *Tractatus Brevis de Deo et Homine, ejusque Felicitate* (a short treatise on God, man and his well-being), in search of a method of thinking that was to become peculiarly

Spinozistic and the first expression of his fundamental principles.

Throughout his life he was a poor man. Lens-grinding was not a profitable business. Moreover, predisposed as Spinoza was to tuberculosis, he was not fitted for work which kept him closely confined to an attic room, his lungs breathing air filled with glass dust. Other men of his age would marry and raise a family. But Johann Rieuwertz, Spinoza's publisher, suggests that the philosopher "never had any inclinations toward matrimony;" and Jean Maximilian Lucas in *The Oldest Biography of Spinoza,* edited by Prof. Abraham Wolf, adds, "although not one of those austere people who look upon marriage as a hindrance to the activities of the mind, he nevertheless did not enter into its bonds . . . perhaps because the love of philosophy absorbed him completely."

Evidently, Spinoza was able to sublimate his sexual urges. The layman, at least, however much interested in psychoanalysis, will have the greatest difficulties detecting in Spinoza's writings signs of sexual frustration. There is a passage in *The Ethics* in which he refers to the genitals as "the parts of shame."[13] Yet this appears to be the typical language of his time, and at the end of *The Ethics* (Part V), he defines "lust" in almost Freudian terms, devoid of any moralistic evaluation.

In 1661, Spinoza moved to Rhijnsburg, a small town near Leyden where he stayed for two years. Rhijnsburg is a beautiful place with low brick houses covered with tiles, a market square, the Rhijn, a tributary of the Rhine flowing through the center of the town, open fields, farm homes and flower gardens all around. The memory of his sojourn here is still preserved in the name "Spinoza Laan",

[13] *Ibid.,* Vol. II, p. 154.

a little side-street. At its end, bordering the fields, there stood a small house in which Spinoza had found lodging. Today it is a museum dedicated to his memory. There is a tablet in front of the house which bears a verse from a hymn of the Collegiants, a body of men and women who without priests or ministers and set forms of ritual tried to live in accordance with the Judeo-Christian ethics. It reads:

> "Ach waren alle Menschen wijs
> En wilden daarbij wel!
> De Aard' waar haar een Paradijs
> Nu is ze meest een Hel."
> (O were all humans wise
> And would they also be well
> The earth would be a paradise
> Now it's mostly a hell.)[14]

Having outlined his philosophy in the *Short Treatise,* Spinoza now proceeded to deduct from the general to the particular. Attempting to explain his objections to Bacon's *Novum Organum* and Descartes' *Discourse on Method,* he set out to write an essay entitled *Tractatus de intellectus emendatione* (On the improvement of the understanding). He begins with these words: "After experience had taught me that all the usual surroundings of social life are vain and futile: seeing that none of the objects of my fears contained in themselves anything either good or bad, except in so far as the mind is affected by them, I finally resolved to inquire whether there might be some real good having power to communicate itself, which would affect the mind singly, to the exclusion of all else; whether, in fact, there

---

[14] In the streetcar from Leyden to Rhijnsburg there is an inscription, also mindful of the Collegiants. It reads: "Spreek vrijmoedig over God maar misbruik nooit Zijn Naam." (Speak freely about God but do not abuse His name.) My translation.

might be anything of which the discovery and attainment would enable me to enjoy continuous, supreme, and unending happiness."[15]

To Francis Bacon, induction was the origin of all truth. Forget the "idols" of things that are not so. Beware of your philosophical desire to put order and regularity in the world. Submit to patient experiment. Observe the facts of nature. Then, if you must, formulate laws or, to use a Platonic term, forms. Spinoza could well appreciate the value of empiric observation. He, too, tried his hand every so often at experiments of a scientific nature. In fact, Gottfried Wilhelm Leibnitz, who borrowed heavily from Spinoza's *Ethics* without ever acknowledging his indebtedness, appears to have made his first contact with Spinoza to discuss some optical problems with him. Though Spinoza realized the importance of physical facts, he also knew the limitation of empirical theories. Conceiving all actual and potential existence as a vast unity, an infinite universe operating in accordance with eternal and immutable laws, the whole direction of inductive reasoning seemed to Spinoza inappropriate. For one thing, how in this infinite universe with an infinite number of particular facts could one hope to observe enough to arrive at safe conclusions? For another thing, while empiric observation might gauge in fairly accurate terms the quantity of certain objects, how could it ever gauge their quality, their "essential" value? To Spinoza, the surer way of attaining truth appeared to be what he called "clear ideas", some fundamental hypotheses which, if borne out by logical reasoning, would lead to further postulates.

"We deduce one thing from another as follows: when we clearly perceive that we feel a certain body and no

[15] *Ibid.*, Vol. II, p. 3.

other, we thence clearly infer that the mind is united to the body, and that their union is the cause of the given sensation; but we cannot thence absolutely understand the nature of the sensation and the union. Or, after I have become acquainted with the nature of vision, and know that it has the property of making one and the same thing appear smaller when far off than when near, I can infer that the sun is larger than it appears, and can draw other conclusions of the same kind.

"Lastly, a thing may be perceived solely through its essence; when, from the fact of knowing something, I know what it is to know that thing, or when, from knowing the essence of the mind, I know that it is united to the body. By the same kind of knowledge we know that two and three make five, or that two lines each parallel to a third, are parallel to one another, etc. The things which I have been able to know by this kind of knowledge are as yet very few.

"In order that the whole matter may be put in a clearer light, I will make use of a single illustration as follows. Three numbers are given—it is required to find a fourth, which shall be to the third as the second is to the first. Tradesmen will at once tell us that they know what is required to find the fourth number, for they have not yet forgotten the rule which was given to them arbitrarily without proof by their masters; others construct a universal axiom from their experience with simple numbers, where the fourth number is self-evident, as in the case of 2,4,3,6; here it is evident that if the second number be multiplied by the third, and the product divided by the first, the quotient is 6; when they see that by this process the number is produced which they knew beforehand to be the proportional, they infer that the process always holds good for finding a fourth number proportional.

Mathematicians, however, know by the proof of the nineteenth proposition of the seventh book of Euclid, what numbers are proportionals, namely, from the nature and property of proportion it follows that the product of the first and fourth will be equal to the product of the second and third: still they do not see the adequate proportionality of the given numbers, or, if they do see it, they see it not by virtue of Euclid's proposition, but intuitively, without going through any process."[16]

There are three kinds of knowledge: a. opinion which may be a cause of error; b. rational knowledge, consisting of "adequate" ideas of the particular properties of things; c. intuitive knowledge, which is philosophic rather than scientific knowledge, synthesis rather than description and analysis. Intuitive knowledge is what the ancients called wisdom. But significant as sound intuition may be, the question is: what are the criteria of such intuitional knowledge? Spinoza tried hard to establish them. He wrote and rewrote the pages of the essay. Finally, he left it as a fragment hoping to return to it in the future. To some extent he did return to it in *The Ethics*.

The quiet and peace which he had enjoyed at first cannot have lasted very long. In the nearby University of Leyden, professors and students soon discovered that there was a man in Rhijnsburg who knew Hebrew better than any of them and who also seemed to be familiar with "the new philosophy" which was then in vogue in academic circles, the cogito ergo sum of Descartes. One of the students, a young man named Albert Burgh, left the university altogether and asked Spinoza to accept him for private tutoring. From the exchange of letters between Simon de Vries, a young merchant and admirer of Spinoza in Amsterdam, and the philosopher, we know not only that

[16] *Ibid.*, Vol. II, pp. 9-10.

Burgh even moved into Spinoza's home but also that Spinoza was not too pleased with his student. The following are pertinent excerpts.

Simon de Vries to Spinoza:

"Most Honourable Friend,—I have for a long time wished to be present with you; but the weather and the hard winter have not been propitious to me. I sometimes complain of my lot, in that we are separated from each other by so long a distance. Happy, yes most happy is the fellow-lodger, abiding under the same roof with you, who can talk with you on the best of subjects, at dinner, at supper, and during your walks. However, though I am far apart from you in body, you have been very frequently present to my mind, especially in your writings, while I read and turn them over."[17]

Spinoza to Simon de Vries:

"Respected Friend,—I have received your long wished-for letter, for which, and for your affection towards me, I heartily thank you. Your long absence has been no less grievous to me than to you; yet in the meantime I rejoice that my trifling studies are of profit to you and our friends. For thus while you are away, I in my absence speak to you. You need not envy my fellow-lodger. There is no one who is more displeasing to me, nor against whom I have been more anxiously on my guard; and therefore I would have you and all my acquaintance warned not to communicate my opinions to him, except when he has come to maturer years. So far he is too childish and inconstant, and is fonder of novelty than of truth. But I hope, that in a few years he will amend these childish faults. Indeed I am almost sure of it, as far as I can judge from his nature. And so his temperament bids me like him."[18]

[17] *Ibid.*, Vol. II, pp. 309-310.
[18] *Ibid.*, Vol. II, pp. 313-314.

During the Rhijnsburg period, Spinoza also came to know Henry Oldenburg, a German diplomat in England who shortly after their first meeting became one of the secretaries of the Royal Society in London. The exchange of letters between Spinoza and Oldenburg, covering fifteen years, from 1661 to 1676, constitutes a most valuable commentary on both *The Ethics* and the *Tractatus Theologico Politicus*.

All available accounts indicate that Spinoza, though but thirty years of age, was by now a rather famed person. When after two years of residence in Rhijnsburg, he moved to Voorburg near The Hague, a brief detour via Amsterdam must have shown him that he had quite a few loyal disciples, men and women who had even formed a club to study his views and who clamored for their publication.

It was on their insistence that he left with Lodwijk Meyer, a physician and Latinist and Rieuwertz, the publisher, his *Geometric Version of Descartes' Philosophy*, with the appendix containing the "Metaphysical Cogitations." No sooner was the book published in Latin than a Dutch translation came on the market. "Had he gone no further," writes Colero, "he might have preserved to this day the deserved Reputation of a Wise and learned Philosopher." The intellectual leaders of the time, foremost among them Huyghens, considered it an honor to frequent his small and bare room. The "Israelite of Voorburg" or "Juif Protestant" (the Reform Jew) as some of them called Spinoza, also attracted the most critical thinkers in the government of Holland. Johann Hudde, for many years mayor of Amsterdam, and Jan de Witt, the Grand Pensionary, were in his circle of friends. He could have easily given up his lens grinding had he been willing to accept financial aid. It is known that Simon de Vries offered him an annual stipend of 2000 florins. But Spinoza politely refused to accept any gifts. Colero informs us that though "he was often invited to eat with his friends, he chose rather to live upon what he had at home, though it were ever so little, than to sit down at a good table at the expense of another man."

On February 16, 1673, Lewis Fabritius, in the name of the Elector Palatine, offered Spinoza the post of professor of philosophy at Heidelberg University under very liberal conditions. This is the letter of invitation:

"Most renowned Sir,—His Most Serene Highness the Elector Palatine, my most gracious master, commands me to write to you, who are, as yet unknown to me, but most favourably regarded by his Most Serene Highness, and to inquire of you, whether you are willing to accept an ordinary professorship of Philosophy in his illustrious university. An annual salary would be paid to you, equal to that enjoyed at present by the ordinary professors. You will hardly find elsewhere a prince more favourable to distinguished talents, among which he reckons yourself. You will have the most ample freedom in philosophical teaching, which the prince is confident you will not misuse, to disturb the religion publicly established. I cannot refrain from seconding the prince's injunction. I therefore most earnestly beg you to reply as soon as possible, and to address your answer either under cover to the Most Serene Elector's resident at the Hague, Mr. Grotius, or to Mr. Gilles Van der Hele, so that it may come in the packet of letters usually sent to the court, or else to avail yourself of some other convenient opportunity for transmitting it. I will only add, that if you come here, you will live pleasantly a life worthy of a philosopher, unless events turn out quite contrary to our expectation and hope. So farewell. I remain, illustrious Sir, Your devoted admirer, I. Lewis

Fabritius. Professor of the Academy of Heidelberg, and Councillor of the Elector Palatine."[19]

The University of Heidelberg, 300 years before Hitlerism destroyed German academic life, was among the outstanding universities of Europe, and the offer coming to the son of Portuguese-Jewish refugees, at a time when Jews were excluded from the faculties of European universities, constituted undoubtedly a signal honor.

Spinoza fully deserved this honor, and it was not false modesty which prevented him from accepting the chair. "One who despises himself", he had written, "is nearest to a vain man." But there was a sentence in the letter which caused Spinoza to say "no." It was the reference to the publicly established religion in the Palatinate and the hope that the philosopher would say and write nothing which might upset the official applecart. This sentence and its implication were not to his taste. He, therefore, answered:

"Distinguished Sir,—If I had ever desired to take a professorship in any faculty, I could not have wished for any other than which is offered to me, through you, by His Most Serene Highness the Elector Palatine, especially because of that freedom in philosophical teaching, which the most gracious prince is kind enough to grant, not to speak of the desire which I have long entertained, to live under the rule of a prince, whom all men admire for his wisdom.

"But since it has never been my wish to teach in public, I have been unable to induce myself to accept this splendid opportunity, though I have long deliberated about it. I think, in the first place, that I should abandon philosophi-

---

[19] *Ibid.*, Vol. II, pp. 373-374. It is possible that Chevreau, in spite of his name an Englishman by birth, scientist and poet by inclination, may have suggested Spinoza's name to the Elector Palatine on one of his frequent trips to the continent.

cal research if I consented to find time for teaching young students. I think, in the second place, that I do not know the limits, within which the freedom of my philosophical teaching would be confined, if I am to avoid all appearance of disturbing the publicly established religion. Religious quarrels do not arise so much from ardent zeal for religion, as from men's various dispositions and love of contradiction, which causes them to habitually distort and condemn everything, however rightly it may have been said. I have experienced these results in my private and secluded station, how much more should I have to fear them after my elevation to this post of honor.

"Thus you see, distinguished Sir, that I am not holding back in the hope of getting something better, but through my love of quietness, which I think I can in some measure secure, if I keep away from lecturing in public."[20]

Spinoza had gone farther than Pastor Colero would have liked him to go. While he continued to grind his lenses during the day, he spent his nights writing his masterwork, *The Ethics*. At the time he had arrived in Voorburg, only a portion of the book had been written. Two years later the fourth part, entitled "Of human bondage", neared completion. Then, suddenly, he stopped.

When, in 1664, the Dutch possessions in North America were captured by the British and a costly war broke out between Holland and England, the liberals, who had come into office in 1653, lost their power in Holland. After the first defeat of the Dutch navy, in June 1665, hysteria swept over the country. Jan de Witt, who had managed to keep the clergy out of politics, was now attacked by them as one who by opening the floodgates to "free-thinking" and "atheism" had brought about the political ruin of Holland. In Voorburg the task of choosing a new pastor

[20] *Ibid.*, Vol. II, pp. 374-375.

had divided the population into two camps. Since the liberal elements were headed by Daniel Tydemann, Spinoza's landlord, their opponents charged them with being under the influence "of a certain Spinoza, a Jew by birth, an atheist, a scoffer at religion and a tool for evil in the republic."

In *The Ethics* Spinoza had written:

"He, who lives under the guidance of reason, endeavours, as far as possible, to render back love, or kindness, for other men's hatred, anger, contempt, etc., towards him. Proof.—All emotions of hatred are bad (IV.xlv.Coroll.i.); therefore he who lives under the guidance of reason will endeavour, as far as possible, to avoid being assailed by such emotions (IV.xix.); consequently, he will also endeavour to prevent others being so assailed (IV. xxxvii.). But hatred is increased by being reciprocated, and can be quenched by love (III.xliii.), so that hatred may pass into love (III.xliv.); therefore he who lives under the guidance of reason will endeavor to repay hatred with love, that is, with kindness.

"Note—He who chooses to avenge wrongs with hatred is assuredly wretched. But he, who strives to conquer hatred with love, fights his battle in joy and confidence; he withstands many as easily as one, and has very little need of fortune's aid. Those whom he vanquishes yield joyfully, not through failure, but through increase in their powers; all these consequences follow so plainly from the mere definitions of love and understanding, that I have no need to prove them in detail."[21]

But apparently there came a point when Spinoza felt that he had to fight back. Bigotry was closing in, and Holland, the one country of Europe which had been free of intolerance, seemed to be destined to join the vast camp

[21] *Ibid.,* Vol. II, p. 220.

of barbarism. Knowing the Bible as few of his contemporaries and realizing that this book had for no good reason become the source of most of the superstitions rampant in the country, he took to writing his *Tractatus Theologico Politicus* (A Theologico-Political Treatise) with the significant subtitle:

"Containing certain discussions wherein is set forth that freedom of thought and speech not only may, without prejudice to piety and the public peace, be granted; but also may not, without danger to piety and the public peace, be withheld."

His friend Oldenburg, puzzled about the interruption of *The Ethics* and Spinoza's new venture, wrote him in September 1665:

"I see that you are engaged not so much in philosophy as in theology, if I may say so. That is, you are recording your thoughts about angels, prophecy, and miracles, but you are doing this, perhaps, in a philosophical manner; however that may be, I am certain that the work is worthy of you, and that I am most anxious to have it. Since these most difficult times prevent free intercourse, I beg at least that you will not disdain to signify to me in your next letter your design and aim in this writing of yours.

"Here we are daily expecting news of a second naval battle, unless indeed your fleet has retired into port. Virtue, the nature of which you hint is being discussed among your friends, belongs to wild beasts not to men. For if men acted according to the guidance of reason, they would not so tear one another in pieces, as they evidently do. But what is the good of my complaining? Vices will exist while men do; but yet they are not continuous, but compensated by the interposition of better things."[22]

Spinoza replied:

[22] *Ibid.*, Vol. II, p. 289.

"I am motivated: 1. By the prejudices of the theologians. These prejudices are among the chief obstacles preventing men from directing their minds to philosophy, and I must therefore, dedicate myself to the task of exposing them . . . 2. The opinion held by the common people who do not cease to accuse me of atheism, and I consider myself compelled to defend myself against this opinion. 3. The freedom of philosophizing and of saying what we think. This freedom I want to vindicate in every possible way since due to the excessive authority and impudence of the preachers it is suppressed here . . ."[23]

Much of the work is today taken for granted. There are few books on religion or politics that do not at least pay lip service to some of the ideas laid down by Spinoza in his *Theologico-Political Treatise*. But to gauge their value, one has to remember that in Spinoza's days witches were being burnt at the stake and men were called atheists if they conceived of God as a divine process permeating the whole universe rather than a being in human form with a long beard throning in the skies. Here was a man about the middle of the seventeenth century who applied the criteria of reason to all religious faiths, who subjected them to a pragmatic test, who refused to accept doctrines that are detrimental to human brotherhood, and who refused to believe that the Bible—Old or New Testament—was literally the revealed word of God. Here was a man whose writings were, in the words of Korthold, "full of thorns."

When the book was published in 1670, a storm broke loose. The Synod of North and South Holland condemned it and urged its suppression by pastors and magistrates. The professors of theology in the leading universities of Holland and Germany joined the chorus of the less learned

[23] Letter No. 30, Spinoza Briefwechsel (ed. Carl Gebhardt) Leipzig 1914. Verlag von Felix Meiner, pp. 141-142 (My translation).

in denouncing it as a "blasphemous", "godless", "impudent" treatise.

"One may very well doubt," declared Dr. Musaeus, professor of divinity at Jena University, "whether among all the men whom the Devil has hired to overthrow all human and divine right, any of them has been more busy about it than that imposter who was born to the great mischief of Church and State." And one may very well add that Herr Dr. Musaeus would be absolutely dead today, had not his tirade against Spinoza kept his name alive in the biographies of the Jewish lensgrinder of Holland. Even our good Pastor Colero had a rash of pious wrath when describing the Theologico-Political Treatise. This was his comment: "The Lord confound thee, Satan, and stop thy mouth!"

Spinoza was in bad health. His friends, who also feared for his safety in Voorburg, had urged him to move into the capital. He found an attic room and board in a house which was then on a back wharf called Stille Veerkade, the same house in which Colero took lodgings some twenty years later when he became pastor of the local Lutheran church and wrote in his spare time the biographical sketch which furnished the raw material of all later biographies of Spinoza—this one included. Simon de Vries, who had died in 1667, had remembered Spinoza in his will, leaving him a legacy of 500 florins a year. It was not a large sum. Yet Spinoza insisted that it was too much for him, and he refused to accept more than 300 florins which he claimed covered all his needs. But apparently the 300 florins were not enough. For in spite of the fact that he continued to work at his trade, he soon looked for cheaper quarters. He felt that he could save money by preparing his own meals, and accordingly he moved to what is now the Domus Spinozana on Paviljoens-gragt, where the landlords were satisfied to take him just as a lodger. There was no stove in his attic chamber. During the winter months Spinoza put on all the clothing he had, kindled the candles on the table and wrote. Curiously enough, his saintlike personality prevented the mob from ever attacking him physically. He had intended his treatise only for the "philosophical reader." As he wrote in the preface:

"To the rest of mankind I care not to commend my treatise, for I cannot expect that it contains anything to please them: I know how deeply rooted are the prejudices embraced under the name of religion; I am aware that in the mind of the masses superstition is no less deeply rooted than fear; I recognize that their constancy is mere obstinacy, and that they are led to praise or blame by impulse rather than reason. Therefore the multitude, and those of like passions with the multitude, I ask not to read my book; nay, I would rather that they should utterly neglect it, than that they should misinterpret it after their wont. They would gain no good themselves, and might prove a stumbling-block to others, whose philosophy is hampered by the belief that Reason is a mere handmaid of Theology, and whom I seek in this work especially to benefit."[24]

But to those who he hoped could read and understand what he had to say, he addressed himself with these words:

"I have often wondered, that persons who make a boast of professing the Christian religion, namely, love, joy, peace, temperance, and charity to all men, should quarrel with such rancorous animosity, and display daily towards one another such bitter hatred, that this, rather than the virtues they claim, is the readiest criterion of their faith. Matters have long since come to such a pass, that one can only pronounce a man Christian, Turk, Jew or Heathen, by his general appearance and attire, by his frequenting this or that place of worship, or employing the phraseology

[24] *Ibid.*, Vol. I, p. 11.

of a particular sect—as for manner of life, it is in all cases the same. Inquiry into the cause of this anomaly leads me unhesitatingly to ascribe it to the fact, that the ministries of the Church are regarded by the masses merely as dignities, her offices as posts of emolument—in short, popular religion may be summed up as respect for ecclesiastics. The spread of this misconception inflamed every worthless fellow with an intense desire to enter holy orders, and thus the love of diffusing God's religion degenerated into sordid avarice and ambition. Every church became a theatre, where orators, instead of church teachers, harangued, caring not to instruct the people, but striving to attract admiration, to bring opponents to public scorn, and to preach only novelties and paradoxes, such as would tickle the ears of their congregation. This state of things necessarily stirred up an amount of controversy, envy, and hatred, which no lapse of time could appease; so that we can scarcely wonder that of the old religion nothing survives but its outward forms (even these, in the mouth of the multitude, seem rather adulation than adoration of the Deity), and that faith has become a mere compound of credulity and prejudices—aye, prejudices too, which degrade man from rational being to beast, which completely stifle the power of judgment between true and false, which seem, in fact, carefully fostered for the purpose of extinguishing the last spark of reason! Piety, great God! and religion are become a tissue of ridiculous mysteries; men, who flatly despise reason, who reject and turn away from understanding as naturally corrupt, these, I say, these of all men, are thought, O lie most horrible! to possess light from on High. Verily, if they had but one spark of light from on High, they would not insolently rave, but would learn to worship God more wisely, and would be as marked among their fellows for mercy as they now are for malice; if they were concerned for their opponents' souls, instead of for their own reputations, they would no longer fiercely persecute, but rather be filled with pity and compassion.

"Furthermore, if any Divine light were in them, it would appear from their doctrine. I grant that they are never tired of professing their wonder at the profound mysteries of Holy Writ; still I cannot discover that they teach anything but speculations of Platonists and Aristotelians, to which (in order to save their credit for Christianity) they have made Holy Writ conform; not content to rave with the Greeks themselves, they want to make the prophets rave also; showing conclusively, that never even in sleep have they caught a glimpse of Scripture's Divine nature. The very vehemence of their admiration for the mysteries plainly attests, that their belief in the Bible is a formal assent rather than a living faith: and the fact is made still more apparent by their laying down beforehand, as a foundation for the study and true interpretation of Scripture, the principle that it is in every passage true and divine."[25]

But Spinoza had preached to deaf ears, and "those of like passions with the multitude" accused him of being a godless man and, indeed, the devil in human incarnation. How this "godless" man lived, has been described by Colero in these words: "One day his landlady asked him if he believed that she could find salvation in the religious faith which she confessed. Whereupon he answered, 'Your religion is good. You do not need to seek another faith nor to have any doubts provided you surrender to God and lead a peaceful and decent life...'"

"It is scarce credible how sober and frugal he was all the time ... It appears ... that he lived a whole day upon a Milk-soup done with Butter, which amounted to three

[25] *Ibid.*, Vol. I, pp. 6-8.

pence, and upon a Pot of Beer of three half pence. Another day he (would) eat nothing but Gruel done with Raisins and Butter, and that dish cost him four pence half penny . . . As for his clothing, he seemed not to care at all. He was dressed like the poorest citizens." But as Lucas informs us, when others were in need, Spinoza would share with them with so much generosity as though he were well-to-do. It was obviously not stinginess that prompted him to live as he did. The rules which he had established for the life of "philosophical" men in his fragmentary essay *On the improvement of the understanding,* were his own rules.

"I. To speak in a manner intelligible to the multitude, and to comply with every general custom that does not hinder the attainment of our purpose. For we can gain from the multitude no small advantages, provided that we strive to accommodate ourselves to its understanding as far as possible: moreover, we shall in this way gain a friendly audience for the reception of the truth.

II. To indulge ourselves with pleasures only in so far as they are necessary for preserving health.

III. Lastly, to endeavour to obtain only sufficient money or other commodities to enable us to preserve our life and health, and to follow such general customs as are consistent with our purpose."[26]

Having spoken out for freedom of thought in the treatise on theology and politics, Spinoza returned to *The Ethics,* his most outstanding work. When, in 1675, the book was finished, he added this note:

"I have thus completed all I wished to set forth touching the mind's power over the emotions and the mind's freedom. Whence it appears, how potent is the wise man, and how much he surpasses the ignorant man, who is driven only by his lusts. For the ignorant man is not only dis-

[26] *Ibid.,* Vol. II, p. 7.

tracted in various ways by external causes without ever gaining the true acquiescence of his spirit, but moreover lives, as it were unwitting of himself, and of God, and of things, and as soon as he ceases to suffer, ceases also to be.

"Whereas the wise man, in so far as he is regarded as such, is scarcely at all disturbed in spirit, but, being conscious of himself, and of God, and of things, by a certain eternal necessity, never ceases to be, but always possesses true acquiescence of his spirit.

"If the way which I have pointed out as leading to this result seems exceedingly hard, it may nevertheless be discovered. Needs must it be hard, since it is so seldom found. How would it be possible, if salvation were ready to our hand, and could without great labour be found, that it should be by almost all men neglected? But all things excellent are as difficult as they are rare."[27]

Though he was not averse to sharing his ideas with others, he decided not to publish the book. His reasons are contained in the following letter to Oldenburg:

"Distinguished and Illustrious Sir,—When I received your letter of the 22nd July, I had set out to Amsterdam for the purpose of publishing the book I had mentioned to you. While I was negotiating, a rumour gained currency that I had in the press a book concerning God, wherein I endeavoured to show that there is no God. This report was believed by many. Hence certain theologians, perhaps the authors of the rumour, took occasion to complain of me before the prince and the magistrates; moreover, the stupid Cartesians, being suspected of favouring me, endeavoured to remove the aspersion by abusing everywhere my opinions and writings, a course which they still pursue. When I became aware of this through trustworthy men, who also assured me that the theologians were everywhere lying in

[27] *Ibid.*, Vol. II, pp. 270-271.

wait for me, I determined to put off publishing till I saw how things were going, and I proposed to inform you of my intentions. But matters seem to get worse and worse, and I am still uncertain what to do.

"Meanwhile I do not like to delay any longer answering your letter. I will first thank you heartily for your friendly warning, which I should be glad to have further explained, so that I may know, which are the doctrines which seem to you to be aimed against the practice of religion and virtue. If principles agree with reason, they are, I take it, also most serviceable to virtue. Further, if it be not troubling you too much I beg you to point out the passages in the *Tractatus Theologico-Politicus* which are objected to by the learned, for I want to illustrate that treatise with notes, and to remove if possible the prejudices conceived against it. Farewell."[28]

Apart from revising the *Tractatus Theologico-Politicus* he had plans for a treatise on the rainbow which was undoubtedly inspired by his craft. He also began writing a manual on Hebrew grammar which he felt was necessary for a better understanding of the Old Testament. According to Colero, he must have intended to add to the manual a complete translation of the Old Testament into Dutch. But when he felt that the Prince of Orange was about to bring ruin to the land of his birth, he again set out to enter the political field by publishing his *Tractatus Politicus,* "Wherein is demonstrated, how the society in which monarchical dominion finds place, as also that in which the dominion is aristocratic, should be ordered, so as not to lapse into a tyranny, but to preserve inviolate the peace and freedom of the citizens."

When he came to Chapter XI, entitled "Of Democracy," he halted. He was too ill to go on. Sensing that his death

[28] *Ibid.,* Vol. II, pp. 296-297.

was near, he authorized Rieuwertz to publish *The Ethics* after his death, but without mentioning the author's name. He knew that it was his life work but he saw no reason for the praise of posterity. He burnt whatever he had written of the translation of the Pentateuch and distributed his library among his friends.

On Saturday, February 21, 1677 he went down to the living room of his landlord to smoke a pipe and to chat with the people of the house. Dr. Meyer, his physician and disciple, came to see him. He ordered a special lunch for Spinoza and put him to bed. A little later when the landlord climbed up to the attic to resume the conversation with his lodger, Baruch Spinoza was dead. He had peacefully passed away at the age of 44, the very same age at which some 200 years later another great Jewish thinker, Theodor Herzl, architect of the new commonwealth of Israel, was to die.

Spinoza's Metaphysics

IT IS NO EASY TASK to compress within a small volume the essentials of any man's thinking. This is particularly true if this man was a Spinoza who preoccupied himself throughout his life with fundamental ideas and who shunned deliberately the discussion of what seemed to him irrelevant observations, bounded by time and locale. It is an almost hopeless venture to reconstruct the general physical and mental atmosphere which prevailed some 300 years ago, when Spinoza wrote the *Ethics*, the *Theological-Political Treatise*, and the *Political Treatise* in his native Holland. No one can determine with certainty what Spinoza treated as evidence and how he glued his facts together. However, his way of reasoning is known to us from his own definitions. These definitions characterize his speculative temper, his predilection for metaphysics, the inquiry into the nature of ultimate reality. They reveal his desire for a unitary view of the world and of man's place in it.

It has become fashionable to dismiss all metaphysical systems as mere "armchair" philosophies which cannot possibly advance the frontiers of knowledge. It is reasoned that only by experiment and careful observation can anything be learned about the actual world of ours. This empiricism, which has its roots in Locke and Hume, who, it might be noted, were themselves "armchair" philosophers, has led to various specialized and undoubtedly valuable scientific endeavors. It has warned us to distinguish between "mere notions", subjective fictions of thought, and observable facts. It has focused on the problem of whether there exists any knowledge independent of experience and our sense perceptions. In concluding that metaphysical questions lie outside the scope of the positivist sciences, the empiricists see no sense in pondering the beginnings and purpose of the world or its creation and a possible creator.

But, curiously enough, these questions persist into our very day. While quite a few people may be satisfied with riding on a train without knowing where it is going, there are still men and women who prefer to have some idea about its starting point, and more important, its direction and destination. They are not deterred by Kant's belief that we can only know phenomena, that is, the things which "appear". There remains the tendency of the human mind, of some human minds at least, to pass beyond the border of experience into the realm of "noumenal" realities, of unconditioned ideas of the universe, of soul and God.

Spinoza's concepts of God and creation are admittedly based on purely *a priori* statements. Anyone who senses only what he can touch with his hands is bound to reject Spinoza's approach to nature and its human component. For this approach involves a system of thought, of logical, "pure reason". Indeed, with the possible exception of Plato, no other philosopher has employed reason and logic as unequivocally, as uncompromisingly, as Spinoza.

David Hume, who owed many of his insights to John Locke, had not yet committed metaphysics "to the flames"; he was not yet insisting on "impressions" as the only acceptable origin of ideas when Spinoza developed his "forms of speculation", to use a Kantian term. Philosophy had not yet acquired the compartmentalized and particularized character which makes it today the poor relative at the table of the academic disciplines. But it is doubtful whether Spinoza would have been convinced by the "common sense" attitude of most of the thinkers of our time and whether he would have refrained today from asking the questions which he asked in the 17th century, questions which continue to propose themselves to reflective people as genuine challenges and for which the experimental method has no answer.

Let it be said at the outset that this chapter on Spinoza's metaphysics does not represent an attempt to review the whole realm of Spinozistic inquiry. It is rather meant to be a reinterpretation of but a few significant Spinozistic theses in the language and thought categories of our time, the middle of the 20th century. In a world that accords saintly character to men like Lenin, Hitler, and Mao Tse Tung; that, in view of the abyss of atomic war, adheres to the self-hypnotic doctrine *"credo quia absurdum est"* (I believe because it is absurd), or trusts in the historical inevitability of the "laws of strife"; in a civilization in which imitation coupled with technical perfection threatens to crowd out inspired individual achievement—under such circumstances any attempt to interest readers in Baruch Spinoza's philosophy may well be considered ludicrous anachronism. Yet the very disillusionments and anxieties which our age produces, necessitate a reexamination of the problems with which Spinoza concerned himself. And if ever a human being could by his teaching inspire fortitude, spiritual discipline and the responsible exercise of conscientious judgment, Spinoza was such a man.

His philosophical and political writings are grounded in his notion of nature, nature as a whole, nature as a unique substance. As soon as we grant him this intuitive "fiction", we shall find his deductions thoroughly intelligible and quite rewarding. If we refuse to probe into expressions like "the universe", "substance", or "creation", his whole structure of the world and of human society becomes rather meaningless. Like Plato, Spinoza conceived of philosophy as the pursuit of wisdom for the sake of the "good life", as the only complete discipline of knowledge in relation to which all other disciplines are subordinate and ancillary. True philosophy to him was the key to the true good, to "a joy continuous and supreme to all eternity." His specific doctrines, such as the sovereign right of every individual to self-preservation or the doctrine of political freedom, cannot be comprehended without an understanding of his metaphysics.

Although he profited from Descartes' *Meditations* and *Discourse on Method*, he was no Cartesian. For he saw serious inconsistencies in Descartes' concepts of the relation of "Thought" and "Extension", of the "Creator" and a "created universe", of "free will" and "necessity". In contrast to Descartes, who seemed to be interested in providing the Catholic Church with quasi-rationalist apologetics for the protection of its doctrines against the revolutionary implications of modern physics, Spinoza, completely fearless, developed a purely intellectual God idea, freed of all traditional connotations, freed particularly of all anthropomorphism. Any mental picture, he realized, must be a mirror of our sense perception, formed by fragments of our experience. But God, he insisted, by His very nature, is outside our experience and cannot, therefore, be described by any imaginative analogy with any phenomena within our experience. Rather He must be conceived, in the geometrical manner, as a succession of propositions and proofs by an effort of "pure reason".

It is not surprising that this unemotional rationalism has earned Spinoza all sorts of abusive epithets by people who have shown no evidence that they ever bothered to study his works seriously and sincerely. While his *a priori* method repelled skeptics like Hume and Voltaire, his interpretation of the Bible antagonized the religiously orthodox. Some have called him a stubborn materialist and determinist who denies all moral values. Others, like Goethe, have seen in him the pantheist who interprets every natural phenomenon as a revelation of God and communicates an almost mystical sense of the unity of the universe. Few have understood him as the most radical reformer in Judaism, as the most outstanding modern Jewish philosopher, standing aside from the main stream of European philosophy and seeking salvation in this world by substituting reason for revelation and for blind obedience to authority without ever surrendering the moral severity which characterizes the prophets, Maimonides and, later on, Moses Mendelssohn, Sigmund Freud, Albert Einstein, indeed, all great Jewish thinkers.

Central to Spinoza's philosophy are his concepts of substance, cause and attribute; these are abstractions which he uses in order to show what he means by God or nature. The traditional doctrine, from Aristotle to Descartes, was that we know the real nature or essence of a substance when we know its essential or necessary attributes. We speak of a tree as having a given size, shape, and color. Some of the qualities or attributes that we include in the description of a particular tree may be secondary or incidental in comparison with other attributes that are primary and without which the object of our description would be no tree. A thing then, be it tree or man, has certain important attributes. Without them there is no such thing. Mathematical physics, stressing quantitative laws in nature, has tended to reduce the catalogue of independent entities characterized by certain qualities which before Galileo were taken for granted in almost any scientific inventory of the universe. Spinoza, inspired as much by the austere monotheistic concept of Judaism as by the modern scientists, argued that the whole notion of a plurality of substances (or nomads as they were called by Leibnitz, his contemporary) involved a logical contradiction. For if the world is conceived to be composed of a plurality of substances, either they must be assumed to be causally related or they must be assumed to be self-created, uncaused, "first causes". But a substance which is not *causa sui*, a cause of itself, a substance which is contingent upon another substance, is a *contradictio in adjecto*. No thing whose qualities and modifications are the products of an interaction with some other unit in the world, no thing that is not a "first cause" conceived through itself, can be called a substance, the attribute of which is always essence, absolute necessity. On the other hand, if we assume the plurality of self-created, self-sufficient substances, God becomes but one of several "first causes", one of many gods, and all His attributes of omnipotence and infinity fall by the wayside.

Indeed, the very notion of a plurality of substances destroys the whole concept of substance. For if we assume the existence of but two substances, as Descartes in his distinction between the mental and the physical world did, either both substances are caused by a force outside of them, which is contrary to the definition of substance as caused by itself, or one is the cause of the other, which again contradicts the definition and makes of substance a finite thing restricted in space and time. Consequently, there can be only one substance which can be defined as *causa sui*, and nothing can exist independent of this one and only substance. This unique substance Spinoza calls *Deus sive Natura*, God or Nature, implying that only God possesses infinite attributes and that nothing else can exist distinguishable from God and capable of delimiting and modifying Him. If only the theologians could have freed themselves from all anthropomorphic and anthropocentric fixations, making of God a sort of super-man throned in the sky, they might have realized that Spinoza had given world humanity the most rational and most unfailing God concept ever conceived in history.

God imagined as Creator in accordance with human ideas of creation and nature, including man, as a product of His "hands", this dualism of artificer and artifact has involved most theologians and metaphysicians in all sorts of insoluble contradictions over the problems of God's freedom of choice, His reasons for creating the actual universe instead of any other possible world, His motives for creating a heaven and a hell, good and evil, etc. If God and nature are assumed to be different substances, caused by themselves, neither God nor nature could be substance, for each is limited by the other. If God is not absolutely and completely identical with nature as a whole, if God is distinguished from nature which He has created, then God cannot be omnipotent and perfect since *ex hypothesi* nature must then possess some qualities which God does not possess; thus God must be a finite and imperfect God.

Moreover, the distinction between Creator and creation makes of God an ephemeral Creator whose creation occurred some 5000 or 8000 or 2 billion years ago and then ceased. If this is the case, if the universe was set in motion by God as the "prime mover" or "first cause", we must regard the universe as a gigantic clock which, once constructed and wound up, operates on its own momentum, except for occasional interferences by the clock maker, interferences which some people like to call miracles. Speaking of the one-time act of creation as a mystery and of startlingly new events as miracles may facilitate the task of certain theologians. But it undermines the concept of God as the eternal and immanent cause of all things, humans among them.

Spinoza's concept of God as the eternal and immanent cause of all existence has been decried as either mystical or unscientific by both the skeptics and the fundamentalists, since he seemed to imply that natural events must be explained as the effect of super-natural causes. Actually, just the reverse is correct; what Spinoza asserts is that natural events cannot be explained by super-natural or transcendent causes. God, to Spinoza, is identical with nature as a whole; and no natural event can be conceived as being outside the all-embracing system of nature.

Deus sive Natura is the only free, self-created cause or, as Spinoza also calls it, *natura naturans,* nature dynamically employing her essential qualities in the various modifications of these qualities. If we think of nature in a given hypothetical moment as the created system, it is *natura naturata,* nature that has been created by God in His complete identity with nature. Both terms, far from being mystical, tell us that whatever exists and happens in the universe belongs to a causal system, that everything ought to be explained, and can ultimately be explained, within a unified science as the effect of some cause.

In Spinoza's view, God as a self-determining substance causes all things to exist, and nothing could have been created in any manner or sequence other than that in which it was actually created. This implies that, in the final analysis, in order to explain why such and such a thing possesses such and such properties, we must deduce these properties from the essential attributes of *Deus sive Natura.*

Here the question arises: can the properties of everything in nature be represented as ultimately accessible to human reason, or must we humans, faced with inexplicable phenomena, in final despair about the limitation of our reasoning capacity, appeal to "revelation"?

Descartes had divided reality into the two independent substances of Thought and Extension. Within the world of Thought, the human mind was conceived to be gifted with immortality, while the human body was conceived to be a perishable part of the system of Extension. Spinoza, having shown that a created substance is a self-contradiction, explained the human mind as part of the infinite intellect of God. While God's mind, or as Aquinas would have said, the Eternal Law, reflects the order of causes in the whole of the universe, the human mind reflects the order of causes in that one tiny part of nature which we call the human body.

Spinoza insists that there are no two different substances as Descartes assumes, those of the mind and the body. Human mind and human body are intertwined; every bodily change is a mental change and vice versa. Every interaction between the human body and its environment is reflected in an idea. But such ideas, derived from sense perception, are uncertain and subjective. Spinoza calls them, in the Platonic tradition, "opinions" and assigns to them a low place in the realm of knowledge. They could also be hallucinations, mistakes in perceptual judgment. He illustrates this point by reminding us of our knowledge of the sun. At the perceptual or empirical level of knowledge, the sun appears to us as a small disc some 500 feet removed from the place on which we stand. When we walk the 500 feet in the direction of the sun, we notice that this disc is quite evasive, that it now appears again to be 500 feet removed from us. It is only on a higher level of knowledge, within an astronomical system of thought, that we realize the sun to be a very huge thing millions of miles away from the earth. It is this scientific level of thinking which alone provides us with adequate knowledge, instead of some *fata morgana,* and if astronomy could ever be merged into an all-inclusive system of logically concatenated ideas, we would also understand why our particular sense perceptions are as inadequate as they actually are.

All our so-called "common sense" knowledge may be discovered to be blooming nonsense after systematic investigation. Even if two or more persons have the same ideas, as long as these ideas are mental images produced by sense perception, nothing is proved except the fact that their bodies had the same or similar experiences. Here, incidentally, is also the first real insight into semantics. For we associate words, written marks or sounds, with certain images that may not be at all free of confusion. To the extent to which human beings are of similar structure and exposed to a similar environment, the formation of their ideas translated into words will be correspondingly similar. But these ideas, based on "common sense" experience, reflect only the transitory impulses of a finite mode of nature, namely man, and do not necessarily reflect the true sequence of causes in the universe as a whole.

Since all bodies are modes of extension and all minds ideas of these modes, there must be some ideas which are common to all men. These ideas common to all men, Spinoza calls *notiones communes,* which, he says, are the beginnings of scientific knowledge. Examples of these common notions are our ideas of motion or of solidity. Mathematics is founded on such common notions. Spinoza's own system of pure reason based on self-evident propositions could be mentioned as another illustration. A common notion conveys a fact which, in the order of the universe, could not be otherwise. Descartes believed he had found what he called a "clear and distinct" idea in the *cogito ergo sum*. I think therefore I am. Having doubted everything, having assumed that extension, motion, and place are but the fictions of the human mind, he came to the conclusion that unless man exists, he could not be deceived; that unless man exists, he could not have thoughts, however deceptive. Having thus established man as a thing which thinks, he concluded that whatever man perceives "clearly and distinctly" is also true. But the consequence of Descartes' metaphysical dualism of Thought and Extension as final substances is that God may after all be a deceiver, that the order of the intellect may not reflect the true order of nature, a position which must lead to total skepticism.

Contrary to Descartes, Spinoza stipulates that truth is the criterion of itself. If in a monistic system like Spinoza's, Thought and Extension are but two attributes of the same unique substance, there can be no malicious deceiver. As mind and body are one, there can be only man's mistaken belief, in the sense that this belief is derived from imagination or mere sense perception. But even such a belief or inadequate idea has its own *ideatum,* its own object, and is necessarily the reflection of some modification of a finite mode in the universe. To say that an idea is false is, in Spinoza's view, to say that it is fragmentary; that it lacks logical relation to other ideas; that it can be corrected if it is linked with other ideas in a larger system of knowledge. While Descartes assumed the human mind to be a free agent with a choice of accepting or rejecting ideas which are "clear and distinct" in the light of reason, Spinoza's metaphysics precludes this sort of "freedom". We can harbor delusions because of confused sense perception or because of a confused association of ideas. But we cannot conceive the sun as a small disc a few hundred feet away from us or accept such a description as adequate if we understand the causes of the particular modification of our body of which this inadequate idea is the reflection. In other words, as soon as we gain scientific knowledge, our knowledge will be on a higher level, reducing false belief, superstition and confusion.

What distinguishes the human being from other animals and inanimate objects is his more complicated organism which, in turn, is able to reflect more of the order of causes in the universe than is open to less complicated organisms. Man, more than any other finite mode within the universe, can acquire knowledge; but only if he were God, only if his body were become identical with nature as a whole, could his mind possess complete knowledge.

For Spinoza, who asserts the union of mind and body, just as Thought and Extension are but two attributes of the same substance, there can logically be no intellectual progress without a corresponding extension of the physical powers of the organism. If a human being has flashes of genuine knowledge, he owes this knowledge not to a mere act of "will", as Descartes would assume, but to complete determination, that is, to his particular situation or constellation as a finite mode in the universe.

From these metaphysical and epistemological concepts, Spinoza deducts his moral system in the *Ethics*. Ethics without metaphysics seemed to him a sheer impossibility. For, if, with Hobbes and other empiricists and nominalists, we deny the validity of metaphysics and, therefore, of any knowledge of ourselves and the world about us, we necessarily lack all standards of truth. We must know our place and potentialities in the universe—*sub specie eternitatis*—before we can arrive at moral precepts.

Man, let us repeat, is a part of nature, a finite mode which like other finite things retains its identity only as long as a certain distribution of motion and rest is preserved within the whole of nature. As by definition the essence of all things is their endeavor (*conatus*) to persist in their own being—Freud calls this libido—man, too, seeks to preserve his personality, his self. Hobbes comes to the same conclusion on the basis of his psychological studies, but there are other psychologists who refute him, due to different experiences and observations. To Spinoza this controversy is irrelevant. For he makes his statement about man's search for self-preservation, not on the basis of any empirical observation of human behavior, but rather by deducing it logically, by "pure reason", from his metaphysical premises. As stated before, he can therefore be refuted only by an attack on his entire system of metaphysics.

In contrast to other animals or so called inanimate things which are less complex in structure, human beings have the God-given capacity of consciousness or mind. Whatever changes there are in the interaction between human beings and between the human and other modes in the universe, changes in vitality or energy are registered in the mind. An increase in vitality produces *laetitia,* that is, joy or pleasure, a sense of perfection; a decrease in vitality produces *tristitia,* pain, a "passion" by which the mind passes to a lower state of perfection. The degree of perfection or power of any finite mode depends on the degree to which it is causally active in relation to the rest of the world. *Deus sive Natura,* being *causa sui,* is causal activity itself. The human being, conceived as a finite mode of both Thought and Extension, has more power when the ideas of his mind are linked together in a causal or scientific system. Vice versa, he has less power when his logical process of thought is disturbed by ideas which are either illogical or the effect of "common sense" perceptions.

In view of Spinoza's emphasis on the union of mind and body, we may infer that an increase in intellectual power must express itself likewise in physical terms, possibly in an internal stability of the organism. The word "express" is in fact somewhat inadequate in this connotation. Spinoza's formulation in the *Ethics* is sharper: "All these considerations clearly show that a mental decision and a bodily appetite, or determined state, are simultaneous, or rather are one and the same thing, which we call decision, when it is regarded under and explained through the attribute of thought, and a conditioned state, when it is regarded under the attribute of extension, and deduced from the laws of motion and rest."[1]

In other words, if a person desires certain things, it is not "free will" which causes this decision but a psychophysical constellation of the human body in the order of the universe. For Descartes and others who believed that such creative activities as the painting of a picture or the writing of a new essay on Spinoza cannot be deduced from purely physical causes, Spinoza has this answer: "No one has hitherto laid down the limits to the powers of the body, that is, no one has as yet been taught by experience what the body can accomplish solely by the laws of nature, in so far as she is regarded as extension. No one hitherto has gained such an accurate knowledge of the bodily mechanism, that he can explain all its functions; nor need I call attention to animals, which far transcend human sagacity, and that somnambulists do many things in their sleep, which they would not venture to do when awake; these instances are enough to show, that the body can by the sole laws of its nature do many things which the mind wonders at . . .

"But, it will be urged, it is impossible that solely from the laws of nature considered as extended substance, we should be able to deduce the causes of buildings, pictures, and things of that kind, which are produced only by hu-

[1] *Ibid.,* Vol. II, p. 134.

man art; nor would the human body, unless it were determined and led by the mind, be capable of building a single temple. However, I have just pointed out that the objectors cannot fix the limits of the body's power, or say what can be concluded from a consideration of its sole nature, whereas they have experience of many things being accomplished solely by the laws of nature, which they would never have believed possible except under the direction of mind: such are the actions performed by somnambulists while asleep, and wondered at by their performers when awake. I would further call attention to the mechanism of the human body, which far surpasses in complexity all that has been put together by human art, not to repeat what I have already shown, namely, that from nature, under whatever attribute she be considered, infinite results follow. As for the second objection, I submit that the world would be much happier, if men were as fully able to keep silence as they are to speak. Experience abundantly shows that men can govern anything more easily than their tongues, and restrain anything more easily than their appetites; when it comes about that many believe, that we are only free in respect to objects which we moderately desire, because our desire for such can easily be controlled by the thought of something else frequently remembered, but that we are by no means free in respect to what we seek with violent emotion, for our desire cannot then be allayed with the remembrance of anything else. However, unless such persons had proved by experience that we do many things which we afterwards repent of, and again that we often, when assailed by contrary emotion, see the better and follow the worse, there would be nothing to prevent their believing that we are free in all things. Thus an infant believes that of its own free will it desires milk, an angry child believes that it freely desires vengeance, a timid child believes that it freely desires to run away; further, a drunken man believes that he utters from the free decision of his mind words which, when he is sober, he would willingly have withheld; thus, too, a delirious man, a garrulous woman, a child, and others of like complexion, believe that they speak from the free decision of their mind, when they are in reality unable to restrain the impulse to talk. Experience teaches us no less clearly than reason, that men believe themselves to be free, simply because they are conscious of their actions, and unconscious of the causes whereby those actions are determined; and further, it is plain that the dictates of the mind are but another name for the appetites, and therefore vary according to the varying state of the body."[2]

Is Spinoza then a materialist? To Hobbes, the world was matter, corporeal, an aggregation of bodies in motion. The materialists of the seventeenth century, continuing to their "spiritual" heirs in our own time, saw the world as a huge mechanical system into which Descartes put the human being as a mysterious, spiritual substance, while other materialists, more given to logic than he, dissolved that spiritual substance likewise into particles of matter.

Spinoza, insisting on the unity of mind and body, is neither materialist nor idealist. He leaves the whole question in abeyance, since he must confess ignorance as to the structure of mind and body. "Again, no one knows how or by what means the mind moves the body, nor how many various degrees of motion it can impart to the body, nor how quickly it can move it. Thus, when men say that this or that physical action has its origin in the mind, which latter has dominion over the body, they are using words without meaning, or are confessing in specious phraseology

[2] *Ibid.,* Vol. II, pp. 132-134.

that they are ignorant of the cause of the said action, and do not wonder at it.

"But, they will say, whether we know or do not know the means whereby the mind acts on the body, we have, at any rate, experience of the fact that unless the human mind is in a fit state to think, the body remains inert. Moreover, we have experience, that the mind alone can determine whether we speak or are silent, and a variety of similar states which, accordingly, we say depend on the mind's decree. But as to the first point, I ask such objectors, whether experience does not also teach, that if the body be inactive the mind is simultaneously unfitted for thinking? For when the body is at rest in sleep, the mind simultaneously is in a state of torpor also, and has no power of thinking, such as it possesses when the body is awake. Again, I think everyone's experience will confirm the statement, that the mind is not at all times equally fit for thinking on a given subject, but according as the body is more or less fitted for being stimulated by the image of this or that object, so also is the mind more or less fitted for contemplating the said object."[3]

All Spinoza can say is that human freedom is limited, because man is a limited, a finite mode; only God, then, has perfect freedom, since God is Nature as a whole. Human emotions, like ambition, lust, anger, jealousy, or fear, arising out of the tendency of self-preservation, actually demonstrate how imperfect our freedom is. We experience these emotions because we are "in many ways driven about by external causes . . . and that, like waves of the sea, driven by contrary winds we toss to and fro unwitting of the issue and of our fate.[4] Only to the extent to which we recognize these emotions, only to the extent to which

[3] *Ibid.*, Vol. II, pp. 132-133.
[4] *Ibid.*, Vol. II, p. 172.

we search for their true causes and abstain from finding specious rationalizations, only to the extent to which we understand and control them, only to that extent can we ever gain freedom.

Excessive self-depreciation and self-destruction are to Spinoza depressed vitality which is completely independent of our conscious will. In this view, moral problems become clinical problems, for there is little sense in any moralistic attitude toward them. The traditional moralist assumes that man is a supernatural being with freedom of choice to choose between good and evil, between a social and an asocial behavior. If a person commits what society calls a crime, the traditional moralist assumes that the criminal could have acted otherwise had he so desired. But the real question is, why did he not desire to act otherwise? The moralist may be quite right in stating that man is normally conscious of his desires. But is he also conscious of the causes which have produced these desires? Spinoza answers that as our physiological and psychological knowledge increases, we shall more and more come to realize not only how causally determined human actions and reactions are, but we shall also realize the conditions under which alternative actions become possible.

At the level of superstition, the burning of a house by lightning is explained as the wrath of God, as His desire to punish its inhabitants for their "sins". As our physical knowledge increases, we discard such supernatural explanations in favor of scientific causation, and we become more able to protect our houses. Since human actions involve a rather complicated order of causes—Professor Einstein once called politics a more difficult discipline than physics—we are, scientifically speaking, still largely inclined to describe most human behavior in terms of inexplicable acts of "will" and "free choice". Only to the extent to which we raise our knowledge from this pre-scientific level of confused ideas can we hope to master our social problems, among others the problem of asocial and criminal behavior.

This does not mean that Spinoza rejects all differences between a piece of rock, a leopard, and a human being. He will readily ascribe consciousness, a mind, and the notion of will and choice to man while denying such consciousness to other animals and inanimate things. "Hence it follows, that the emotions of the animals which are called irrational (for after learning the origin of mind we cannot doubt that brutes feel) only differ from man's emotions, to the extent that brute nature differs from human nature. Horse and man are alike carried away by the desire of procreation; but the desire of the former is equine, the desire of the latter is human. So also the lusts and appetites of insects, fishes, and birds must needs vary according to the several natures. Thus, although each individual lives content and rejoices in that nature belonging to him wherein he has his being, yet the life wherein each is content and rejoices, is nothing else but the idea, or soul, of the said individual, and hence the joy of one only differs in nature from the joy of another, to the extent that the essence of one differs from the essence of another. Lastly, it follows from the foregoing proposition, that there is no small difference between the joy which actuates, say a drunkard, and the joy possessed by a philosopher, as I just mention here by the way."[5]

Anything which obstructs the development of knowledge and intelligence reduces the vitality or freedom of man. Social and political instability are, therefore, a hindrance to man's progress. Those who are interested in the advancement of knowledge must help their fellow men

[5] *Ibid.*, Vol. II, pp. 170-171.

to emancipate themselves from superstition and ignorance which in turn breed hatred and strife. Wise men will repay hatred with understanding and kindliness. They will do so not because of any rewards promised to them in heaven, or because of fear of hell. Heaven and hell are in ourselves; and virtue is its own reward. "A free man thinks of death least of all things." (*Ethics,* Part IV, Prop. LXVII). The more true knowledge man gains, the more he can view himself and other things *sub specie eternitatis,* the more equanimity he will enjoy, the more he will master his fate. The more he understands his urge to self-preservation, the more he understands himself and the rest of nature, the more he will understand God, that is, the eternal order of the universe. This is what Spinoza means by his description of the "good life" as the "intellectual love of God." It is not flight into other-worldly speculations, not an attempt to divorce man from the world of reality. On the contrary, Spinoza's final proof for rationality is to seek and love God; and to seek and love God means to be rational.

Spinoza was never plagued by the desire of certain people for immortality. He remembered from his childhood teachings in the synagogue of Amsterdam the Hebrew words, "Mi afar ata . . . from the dust thou are and to the dust thou wilt return," as well as Maimonides' principle of faith, "I believe with perfect faith that there will be a resurrection of the dead at the time it shall please the Creator, blessed be His name." This is where Spinoza lets the case rest. For how could man know what God has in store for him? For Spinoza to ask the question, When did God come into existence? was as senseless as to ask: When did the three angles of a triangle become equal to two right angles? No human imagination can fully grasp the notion of an eternal substance which is God. It is only by a process of "pure" reasoning as used in geometry that we can arrive at the notion of eternity. As a part of nature, we humans share in this eternity. To the extent to which we attain genuine knowledge, to the extent to which our minds unite with God under the attribute of thought, we gain a glimpse of that eternity. But as finite modes we are dependent on the laws, largely unknown to us, which govern all finite modes, among them the destruction of the human body.

Having established man's place in the universe, Spinoza, at least two hundred years in advance of his age, proceeded to establish reason as a *sine qua non* in politics. Like Hobbes, he asserts that man, for the sake of his self-preservation, in order to gain peace and security, constructs political associations, among them the state. As to the reason, however, which causes man to make peace and security the criteria of his political decisions, Spinoza differs diametrically from Hobbes. According to Hobbes, as later to Rousseau, man is free insofar as he can satisfy his physiologically determined impulses or, to use a Freudian term, as long as he can live in accordance with the "pleasure principle". Having a very pessimistic view of human nature, Hobbes considered peace and security to be a negative condition, an effort on man's part to protect himself from his own brutality and that of his fellow men. Normally all men are Behemoth, mere beasts. They need the Leviathan, the dictatorial state, to hold them *in terrorem*. For Spinoza the use of reason is not merely a means to man's self-preservation as an end. Reason rather constitutes the end itself. The criterion by which he judges a political organization is whether it impedes or develops man's reasoning capacity, which alone can set man free by giving him the necessary insight into the order of nature. While Hobbes' empiricism leads invariably to authoritarianism, Spinoza's metaphysics make him the outstanding and most logical advocate of political democracy, of religious toleration, and of freedom of thought. Where Hobbes is afraid of his fellow men, Spinoza asserts that nothing is so useful to man as other men.

Impelled by his need for union, having become aware of the usefulness of associative life, man builds the state. The criterion of usefulness eliminates the desirability of both the Hobbesian Leviathan and the Lockeian emasculated laissez-faire state. According to Spinoza, no commonwealth is adequate unless it affords its citizens a very real opportunity to use their reasoning capacity. Unlike Hobbes, Spinoza, therefore, would never have compromised with modern totalitarianism, whether in its Fascist or Communist form, since all totalitarianism is by definition and practice inimical to freedom of thought and a creative peace. Nor would he have seen much sense in Locke's wishful thinking about a pre-political state of nature as "a state of perfect freedom" and the Whiggish consequences drawn by Locke for political life. Spinoza realized that outside any organized society man's power and freedom are limited by fear of attack on the part of other men and by inability to supply all one's needs. He also realized that in order to be useful, to assure collective security to its members, the state must have certain enforcement powers to deter and to curb potential aggression. He conceived society as a balance between conflicting forces of self-assertion, and government as the science and art to protect man from both oppression and anarchy.

His *Theologico-Political Treatise,* written as a protest against religious fanaticism and intolerance, has been called the "first document in the modern science of Biblical criticism." It seems to be too modern for some people even in our day. In this treatise, which we shall discuss in greater detail in the next chapter, he asserts that faith and philosophy stand on totally different footings; that religion cannot be endangered by freedom of thought and speech so necessary in scientific and philosophical matters; that the task of religion is to preach and practice justice and charity. But since the book also showed how some of the chief superstitions are at times deliberately fostered by people seeking temporal advantages under the cloak of religion it was banned from circulation by the ecclesiastical authorities.

He could not foresee our time in which the threat to freedom of thought comes, at least in the Western world, no longer from the churches but rather from the extension of political power into all spheres of associative life, from political fanaticism and political demagoguery. Nevertheless, the *Political Treatise,* emphasizing that man's loyalty to the state should be judged, like his loyalty to God, from his actions alone, from his social-mindedness or lack of it, that the best government is government which allows freedom of philosophical speculation no less than freedom of religious belief, constitutes in spite of its fragmentary character a formidable intellectual weapon in the struggle between democracy and totalitarianism.

He did not have to advocate revolution against the Leviathan. To him it was a natural phenomenon that men cannot and will not forever surrender their God-given reasoning capacity; that a state which is not based on the genuine consent of its citizens invites public strife and becomes the author of its own destruction; that where discussion and persuasion are forbidden, human beings will fight with character assassination, fists and guns; that, in the long run, only those states will survive which do not disregard the laws of human nature and which, therefore, enjoy political stability.

Spinoza's Concept of God

THE MEDIEVAL PHILOSOPHERS, foremost among them Maimonides and Thomas Aquinas, had established two criteria for the justification of religion, revelation and reason. Since all reason is ultimately based either on man's experience, that is, his empiric observation or on arbitrarily established axioms, reason can arrive at valid conclusions only if the premises on which it is based are true.

Religion, like mathematics or logic, accepts certain axiomatic premises intuitively. Maimonides and Aquinas were, therefore, right in stating that the very existence of religion implies a human need for faith as well as for reason. Their error consisted in accepting faith in a particular historic setting, be it the Hebrew-Palestinian civilization or the Christian-Roman civilization, as axiomatic and in assuming that the Jewish and Christian traditions had been "revealed" for all times and for all mankind. By their identification of historic and, therefore, time-bound traditions with "eternal truth," they were bound to create a conflict between science and religion, between the Copernican view of the universe and the world picture taught by traditional Judaism and traditional Christendom.

To assign science and religion their proper place in man's existence, to show that in both the realm of religion as well as in the realm of science we learn by trial and error; to bridge the gap between reason and faith; to prove that human life is an integral part of the life of the universe related to all other forms of existence, and that God's purpose is not capricious but manifests itself in natural and moral law, Spinoza wrote the *Theologico-Political Treatise* and *The Ethics*.

Anticipating in great measure the procedures of modern Bible critics, Spinoza first of all examined the theory of the literal inspiration of both testaments. How is it, he asked, that theologians of different religious faiths have different conceptions of God, that even within the same religious tradition different prophets and apostles have conceived of God and His emanations or attributes differently? And this was his answer:

"As the prophets perceived the revelations of God by the aid of imagination, they could indisputably perceive much that is beyond the boundary of the intellect, for many more ideas can be constructed from words and figures than from the principles and notions on which the whole fabric of reasoned knowledge is reared.

"Thus we have a clue to the fact that the prophets perceived nearly everything in parables and allegories, and clothed spiritual truths in bodily forms, for such is the usual method of imagination. We need no longer wonder that Scripture and the prophets speak so strangely and obscurely of God's Spirit or Mind (cf. Numbers xi 17, 1 Kings xxii. 21, &c.), that the Lord was seen by Micah as sitting, by Daniel as an old man clothed in white, by Ezekiel as a fire, that the Holy Spirit appeared to those with Christ as a descending dove, to the apostles as fiery tongues, to Paul on his conversion as a great light."[1]

Imagination does not, in its own nature, involve any certainty of truth. Its content varies with the educational background of those who prophesy.

"Prophecy varied according to the opinions held by the prophets; for instance, to the Magi, who believed in

[1] *Ibid.*, Vol. I, p. 25.

the follies of astrology, the birth of Christ was revealed through the vision of the star in the East. To the augurs of Nebuchadnezzar the destruction of Jerusalem was revealed through entrails, whereas the king himself inferred it from oracles and the direction of arrows which he shot into the air. To prophets who believed that man acts from free choice and by his own power, God was revealed as standing apart from and ignorant of future human actions."[2]

Even the style of prophecy varies in accordance with the eloquence of the individual seer. "The prophecies of Ezekiel and Amos are not written in a cultivated style like those of Isaiah and Nahum, but more rudely. Any Hebrew scholar who wishes to inquire into this point more closely, and compares chapters of the different prophets treating of the same subject, will find great dissimilarity of style. Compare for instance, chap. i. of the courtly Isaiah, verse 11 to verse 20, with chap. v. of the countryman Amos, verses 21-24. Compare also the order and reasoning of the prophecies of Jeremiah, written in Idumaea (chap. xlix.), with the order and reasoning of Obadiah. Compare, lastly, Isa. xl. 19,20 and xliv. 8, with Hosea viii. 6, and xiii. 2. And so on."[3]

Spinoza's conclusion is that prophecy never rendered the prophets more learned "but left them with their former opinions, and that we are, therefore, not at all bound to trust them in matters of intellect."[4]

Even their concept of God is not necessarily binding on later generations. "Adam, the first man to whom God was revealed, did not know that He is omnipotent and omniscient; for he hid himself from Him, and attempted to make

[2] *Ibid.*, Vol. I, p. 30.
[3] *Ibid.*, Vol. I, p. 32.
[4] *Ibid.*, Vol. I, p. 33.

excuses for his fault before God, as though he had had to do with a man . . . Abraham also knew not that God is omnipresent, and has foreknowledge of all things; for when he heard the sentence against the inhabitants of Sodom, he prayed that the Lord should not execute it till He had ascertained whether they all merited such punishment . . . Moses believed that God dwelt in the heavens, God was revealed to him as coming down from heaven on to a mountain, and in order to talk with the Lord Moses went up the mountain, which he certainly need not have done if he could have conceived of God as omnipresent . . .

"Samuel believed that the Lord never repented of anything He had decreed (1 Sam, xv. 29), for when Saul was sorry for his sin, and wished to worship God and ask for forgiveness, Samuel said that the Lord would not go back from his decree. To Jeremiah, on the other hand, it was revealed that, 'If that nation against whom I (the Lord) have pronounced, turn from their evil, I will repent of the evil that I thought to do unto them. If it do evil in my sight, that it obey not my voice, then I will repent of the good wherewith I said I would benefit them' (Jer. xviii, 8-10) . . .

"We can come to no different conclusion with respect to the reasonings of Christ, by which He convicted the Pharisees of pride and ignorance, and exhorted His disciples to lead the true life. He adapted them to each man's opinions and principles. For instance, when he said to the Pharisees (Matt. xii. 26), 'And if Satan cast out devils, his house is divided against itself, how then shall his kingdom stand?' He only wished to convince the Pharisees according to their own principles, not to teach that there are devils, or any kingdom of devils. So, too, when he said to his disciples (Matt. viii. 10), 'See that ye despise not one of these little ones, for I say unto you that their angels,' etc., He merely desired to warn them against pride and despising any of their fellows, not to insist on the actual reason given, which was simply adopted in order to persuade them more easily."[5]

Against more anthropomorphic notions of the Deity, Spinoza sets the idea of God as an Infinite Being, a cosmic process, fulfilling in the uniformity of natural law the perfection of His own nature. To Spinoza God is "natura naturans," nature as it develops by virtue of its own laws and "natura naturata," the cosmos as it has developed.

"By the help of God, I mean the fixed and unchangeable order of nature or the chain of natural events: for I have said before and shown elsewhere that the universal laws of nature, according to which all things exist and are determined, are only another name for the eternal decrees of God, which always involve eternal truth and necessity. So that to say that everything happens according to natural laws, and to say that everything is ordained by the decree and ordinance of God, is the same thing. Now since the power in nature is identical with the power of God, by which alone all things happen and are determined, it follows that whatsoever man, as a part of nature, provides himself with to aid and preserve his existence, or whatsoever nature affords him without his help, is given to him solely by the Divine power, acting either through human nature or through external circumstance. So whatever human nature can furnish itself with by its own efforts to preserve its existence, may be fitly called the inward aid of God, whereas whatever else accrues to man's profit from outward causes may be called the external aid of God."[6]

God is the immanent cause of all existence (Deum rerum omnium causam immanentem), and his omnipresence is

[5] *Ibid.*, Vol. I, pp. 34-41.
[6] *Ibid.*, Vol. I, pp. 44-45.

best understood if we remember that man is an integral part of the process by which the cosmos is evolved. No matter what instruments our intellect may devise to explore the universe, "without God nothing can exist or be conceived,"[7] or to use a rabbinic saying, "No place is void of the Shehinah." (the presence of God). Since the knowledge of an effect through its cause is the same thing as the knowledge of a particular property of a cause, "the greater our knowledge of natural phenomena, the more perfect is our knowledge of the essence of God (which is the cause of all things)."[8]

The word "perfect" means complete, finished. The "perfection" of human effort in building a "perfect" commonwealth, the "perfection" of our knowledge of atomic energy—all this is implied in the concept of God, in the sense that God acts and decrees all things by the necessity of His nature.

Does this concept of God obliterate the distinction between "right" and "wrong," between "good" and "evil"? Does it obey the authority of a divine law? This is Spinoza's reply:

"God commanded Adam not to eat the fruit of the tree of the knowledge of good and evil; this seems to mean that God commanded Adam to do and to seek after righteousness because it was good, not because the contrary was evil: that is, to seek the good for its own sake, not from the fear of evil. We have seen that he who acts rightly from the true knowledge and love of right, acts with freedom and constancy, whereas he who acts from fear of evil, is under the constraint of evil, and acts in bondage under external control. So that this commandment of God to Adam comprehends the whole Divine natural law, and ab-

[7] *Ibid.*, Vol. I, p. 59.
[8] *Idem.*

solutely agrees with the dictates of the light of nature; nay, it would be easy to explain on this basis the whole history or allegory of the first man. But I prefer to pass over the subject in silence, because, in the first place, I cannot be absolutely certain that my explanation would be in accordance with the intention of the sacred writer; and, secondly, because many do not admit that this history is an allegory, maintaining it to be a simple narrative of facts. It will be better, therefore, to adduce other passages of Scripture, especially such as were written by him, who speaks with all the strength of his natural understanding, in which he surpassed all his contemporaries, and whose sayings are accepted by the people as of equal weight with those of the prophets. I mean Solomon, whose prudence and wisdom are commended in Scripture rather than his piety and gift of prophecy. He, in his proverbs calls the human intellect the well-spring of true life, and declares that misfortune is made up of folly. Understanding is a well-spring of life to him that hath it; but the instruction of fools is folly, Prov. xvi. 22. Life being taken to mean the true life (as is evident from Deut. xxx. 19), the fruit of the understanding consists only in the true life, and its absence constitutes punishment. All this absolutely agrees with what was set out in our fourth point concerning natural law. Moreover our position that it is the well-spring of life, and that the intellect alone lays down laws for the wise, is plainly taught by the sage, for he says (Prov. xiii. 14): 'The law of the wise is a fountain of life'—that is, as we gather from the preceding text, the understanding. In chap. iii. 13, he expressly teaches that the understanding renders man blessed and happy, and gives him true peace of mind. 'Happy is the man that findeth wisdom, and the man that getteth understanding,' for 'Wisdom gives length of days, and riches and honour; her ways are ways of pleasantness, and all her paths peace' (xiii. 16,17). According to Solomon, therefore, it is only the wise who live in peace and equanimity, not like the wicked whose minds drift hither and thither, and (as Isaiah says, chap. lvii. 20) 'are like the troubled sea, for them there is no peace . . .'

"Lastly, we must by no mean pass over the passage in Paul's Epistle to the Romans, i. 20, in which he says: 'For the invisible things of God from the creation of the world are clearly seen, being understood by the things that are made, even His eternal power and Godhead; so that they are without excuse, because, when they knew God, they glorified Him not as God, neither were they thankful.' These words clearly show that everyone can by the light of nature clearly understand the goodness and the eternal divinity of God, and can thence know and deduce what they should seek for and what avoid; wherefore the Apostle says that they are without excuse and cannot plead ignorance, as they certainly might if it were a question of supernatural light and the incarnation, passion, and resurrection of Christ."[9]

The attributes commonly ascribed to God are either metaphysical or ethical or both. Realizing that associative life makes certain demands on the individual and that the human being is an animal with socio-political tendencies, we are apt to attribute to God whatever makes for a "good society" on earth. In a sense we project the child-father relationship into our relationship with God. Just as the child needs a strong, reliable, loving father (and is disappointed if his father or mother falls short of his expectations), we believe God to be strong, just, merciful, "good." By worshiping God with moral attributes, we express the belief that He is what men for the sake of their well-being or "salvation" ought to be. Since we cannot accept the idea

[9] *Ibid.*, Vol. I, pp. 65-68.

that God is as imperfect as we are, we add to His ethical attributes of justice and mercy the metaphysical attributes of omnipotence, omniscience, and perfection.

But by ascribing to God both ethical and metaphysical attributes, we involve ourselves in a logical dilemma for which the whole history of theology is a living record. What meaning can there be to God's justice if God is conceived as an omnipotent, personal Being? Does it mean that God administers justice by rewarding the just and punishing the unjust? The book of Job challenges this assumption, and already Abraham, when pleading for Sodom and Gomorrah, asked: "Shall not the judge of all the earth deal justly?"

A rabbinical midrash[10] answers Abraham's question by stating: "The judge of all the world cannot deal out justice." This, as Rabbi Eugene Kohn in *Religion and Humanity* explains, is not a denial of God's existence, but rather a wise interpretation of the fact that the universe, and, therefore, also life on earth, is so interrelated that it is impossible to have the evildoers suffer without involving the righteous in that suffering. Do we not all suffer from the machinations of the Presidium of the Communist party of the Soviet Union, the lynching of a Negro, or the follies of American superpatriots? If God is an omnipresent, omniscient, personal God, all suffering must be caused by His will. And if He is a God of justice, such suffering must be a punishment for evil. Consequently, the righteous, who suffer, must be sinners and the wicked, who get away with murder, must be righteous. Who would be willing to accept this absurdity?

Spinoza solves the contradiction inherent in the concept of God as a transcendent Being with human traits, by con-

[10] Midrash is a commentary on biblical laws, developed between the 2nd and 12th century A.D.

ceiving of God as a cosmic self-fulfillment that makes for the supreme worthiness of life and allows us to describe all constructive, life-giving human qualities such as justice and mercy, as divine, that is, in conformity with the interrelationship of all parts of the universe. What then is the significance of "evil" in the world?

In the Jewish tradition, God is the "Maker of light and the Creator of darkness, Maker of Peace and Creator of evil." (Isaiah 45: 6-7). Though there is evil or the power of destructiveness in the world, this actually represents the unrealized good, a challenge for man as the co-creator with God, a chance for man's "knowledge" to show itself.

Spinoza defines "good" as "that which we certainly know to be useful to us,"[11] and "evil" as "that which we certainly know to be a hindrance to us in the attainment of any good."[12] "As virtue is nothing else but action in accordance with the laws of one's own nature (IV. Def. viii.), and as no one endeavours to preserve his own being, except in accordance with the laws of his own nature, it follows, first, that the foundation of virtue is the endeavour to preserve one's own being, and that happiness consists in man's power of preserving his own being; secondly, that virtue is to be desired for its own sake, and that there is nothing more excellent or more useful to us, for the sake of which we should desire it, thirdly and lastly, that suicides are weak-minded, and are overcome by external causes repugnant to their nature . . .

"To man there is nothing more useful than man—nothing, I repeat, more excellent for preserving their being can be wished for by men, than that all should so in all points agree, that the minds and bodies of all should form, as it were, one single mind and one single body, and that all

[11] *Ibid.*, Vol. II, p. 190.
[12] *Ibid.*, Vol. II, p. 190.

should, with one consent, as far as they are able, endeavour to preserve their being, and all with one consent seek what is useful to them all. Hence, men who are governed by reason—that is, who seek what is useful to them in accordance with reason—desire for themselves nothing, which they do not also desire for the rest of mankind, and, consequently, are just, faithful, and honourable in their conduct . . .

"Such are the dictates of reason, which I purposed thus briefly to indicate, before beginning to prove them in greater detail. I have taken this course, in order, if possible to gain the attention of those who believe, that the principle that every man is bound to seek what is useful for himself is the foundation of impiety, rather than of piety and virtue."[13]

And he continues, "the effort for self-preservation is the essence of a thing; therefore, if any virtue could be conceived as prior thereto, the essence of a thing would have to be conceived as prior to itself, which is obviously absurd."[14]

The human effort for self-preservation is also the foundation of human virtue. It is life giving, constructive and therefore potentially "good." Whenever the mind endeavors to preserve the human personality (or self), its effort at understanding "is the first and single basis of virtue."[15]

Having identified self-preservation with virtue, Spinoza arrives at the famous propositions XXVII and XXVIII of *The Ethics:*

"Prop. XXVII. We know nothing to be certainly good or evil, save such things as really conduce to understanding, or such as are able to hinder us from understanding.

---

[13] *Ibid.,* Vol. II, pp. 201-202.
[14] *Ibid.,* Vol. II, p. 203.
[15] *Ibid.,* Vol. II, p. 205.

"Proof.—The mind, in so far as it reasons, desires nothing beyond understanding, and judges nothing to be useful to itself, save such things as conduce to understanding (by the foregoing Prop.). But the mind (II. xli. xliii. and note) cannot possess certainty concerning anything, except in so far as it has adequate ideas, or (what by II. xl. note, is the same thing) in so far as it reasons.

"Prop. XXVIII. The mind's highest good is the knowledge of God, and the mind's highest virtue is to know God.

"Proof.—The mind is not capable of understanding anything higher than God, that is (I. Def. vi.), than a Being absolutely infinite, and without which (I. xv.) nothing can either be or be conceived; therefore (IV. xxvi. and xxvii.), the mind's highest utility or (IV. Def. i.) good is the knowledge of God. Again, the mind is active, only in so far as it understands, and only to the same extent can it be said absolutely to act virtuously. The mind's absolute virtue is therefore to understand. Now, as we have already shown, the highest that the mind can understand is God; therefore the highest virtue of the mind is to understand or to know God."[16]

Whatever is in harmony with our nature, is "necessarily good."[17] Vice versa, nothing can be good that destroys this harmony. "In so far as men are a prey to passion, they cannot, in that respect, be said to be naturally in harmony."[18] This is self-evident. For "passion" implies something we want but do not have, something which produces in us a tension, the very negation of harmony.

Consequently, "service of God" means to Spinoza the harmonization of men's interests, notwithstanding their diversity. There can be no conflicting "goods," since there

[16] *Ibid.*, Vol. II, pp. 205-206.
[17] *Ibid.*, Vol. II, p. 207.
[18] *Ibid.*, Vol. II, p. 207.

is no multiplicity of gods on whom human self-preservation relies. "Shema Jisrael, Adonaj Elohenu, Adonaj Ehad" (Hear, O Israel, the Lord our God, the Lord is One)—this watchword of the Jewish faith which knows no compromise, was also Spinoza's watchword.

Anticipating the liberal Judaism of our day, Spinoza conceived of this One God as the leitmotif by which the universe gives meaning to man and answers to his need for self-realization. Just as love, loyalty, courage, and similar ideas are personal and yet not persons, God can be conceived as personal, as the sponsor of the human personality, without being identified as a person Himself.

"The narratives in the Old and New Testaments surpass profane history, and differ among themselves in merit simply by reason of the salutory doctrines which they inculcate."[19] But they must be read as history and not as eternally valid "revelation." Indeed, it can be shown, as Spinoza did show, that the first five books of Holy Writ, ascribed to Moses, were written long after Moses' death, probably, as Spinoza assumes, by Ezra in the sixth century B.C., when the Jews upon their return from the Babylonian captivity rebuilt the Temple in Jerusalem and made the study and practice of the Torah (the first five books of the Old Testament) the basis of Jewish communal life.

It can also be demonstrated, as Spinoza demonstrated, that the so-called miracles in both the Old and the New Testament are not essential to religious faith, that they may be the poetic expression of opinions and prejudices of the writers, symbolical and imaginary, as, for instance, that God came down from heaven (Exod. XIX. 28) and that Mount Sinai smoked because God descended upon it surrounded with fire or, again, that Elijah ascended into heaven in a chariot of fire, with horses of fire. Indeed, it

[19] *Ibid.*, Vol. I, p. 79.

could be said that whatever happens in contradiction to the laws of nature "would also be in contravention to the order which God has established in nature for ever through universal natural laws; it would, therefore, be in contravention to God's nature and laws, and, consequently, belief in it would throw doubt upon everything, and lead to Atheism."[20]

Goethe, who took much of his inspiration from Spinoza, formulated this idea in his Orphic Sayings in the following words:

> "According as the sun and planets saw,
> From their bright thrones, the moment of thy birth,
> Such is thy Destiny; and by that Law
> Thou must go on—and on—upon the earth.
> Such must thou be; Thyself thou canst not flee . . ."

The power upon which we humans depend for the realization of our best potentialities, for our harmony with the universe, cannot be a capricious power. While we may not always comprehend God, however much we may try to discover His ways, there would be no sanctity, no holiness in the world if God were chaos. The God of Spinoza is the full, unfettered life, the "soul" of all existence; and "he who clearly and distinctly understands himself and his emotions, loves God, and so much the more in proportion as he more understands himself and his emotions."[21] Man's "freedom" is man's understanding of himself. The Socratic imperative, "know thyself," is for Spinoza the only avenue to human freedom. "A free man is one who lives under the guidance of reason . . . who strives to act, and to live, and to preserve his being on the basis of seeking his own true advantage."[22]

[20] *Ibid.*, Vol. I, p. 87.
[21] *Ibid.*, Vol. II, p. 255.
[22] *Ibid.*, Vol. II, p. 232.

It is this freedom which distinguishes the human being from all other creatures, and which gives us our hope of special "immortality." Suppose man were nothing but a lump of sensitive matter, endowed with a special mechanism called "mind," which combined with a brain, and a voice admittedly gives the life of the human animal a wider scope for development than is enjoyed, let us say, by an acorn. Suppose that man, a given man, from infancy on, is kept in isolation, fed with vitamins and given just the very minimum of attention to keep physically alive. What is there in this conditioned man, isolated from the society of his fellow men, that justifies us in attributing to him a consciousness of his existence and human freedom? If by "immortality" of the "soul" we mean that after the death of the body, the "soul" will survive, what really is there in our specially conditioned, wretched man to guarantee that he will become immortal, while the acorn or a piece of rock will not?

Since the individual personality, whether of a conditioned moron or of the most gifted person, expresses itself invariably through physical organs, the presumption must be against the possibility of a separate immortal "soul." But if we conceive all life as eternal and all the units of the universe, infinite in space and time, as interrelated, we shall understand that but for the acorn or the rock beneath our feet or the fierce leopard in the jungle, we could have no continued existence. And if life, which to Spinoza and all Jews is synonymous with God, dwells in whatever exists, whether we perceive its true form or not, God's breath (in Hebrew: Ruah) is in all His creation—the acorn, the rock, the leopard, the moron, and the wisest man or woman. If by immortality we mean that life is eternal, whatever its vessels, we shall realize that all creation partakes of God's immortality. In this sense no life is rendered futile after death. Or, as Spinoza interprets this idea:

"There is necessarily in God a concept or idea, which expresses the essence of the human body (last Prop.), which, therefore, is necessarily something appertaining to the essence of the human mind and duration, definable by time, except in so far as it expresses the actual existence of the body, which is explained through duration, and may be defined by time—that is (II. viii. Coroll.), we do not assign to it duration, except while the body endures. Yet, as there is something, notwithstanding, which is conceived by a certain eternal necessity through the very essence of God (last Prop.); this something, which appertains to the essence of the mind, will necessarily be eternal.

"This idea, which expresses the essence of the body under the form of eternity, is, as we have said, a certain mode of thinking, which belongs to the essence of the mind, and is necessarily eternal. Yet it is not possible that we should remember that we existed before our body, for our body can bear no trace of such existence, neither can eternity be defined in terms of time, or have any relation to time. But, notwithstanding, we feel and know that we are eternal. For the mind feels those things that it conceives by understanding, no less than those things that it remembers. For the eyes of the mind, whereby it sees and observes things, are none other than proofs. Thus, although we do not remember that we existed before the body, yet we feel that our mind, in so far as it involves the essence of the body, under the form of eternity, is eternal, and that thus its existence cannot be defined in terms of time, or explained through duration."[23] It is quite possible that Jesus' remark, "I and my Father are one" meant exactly what Spinoza tries to convey, namely, that the entry

[23] *Ibid.*, Vol. II, pp. 259-260.

into eternal life was not the particular affair of a particular personal entity, but rather the dissolution of the human form known to us as Jesus of Nazareth into the unfettered life, the soul of all existence, past, present and future, which is God.

This God-concept knows no "chosen people," no "select" group. Every Sabbath morning, as long as Jews have congregated in synagogues and temples, the scroll of the Torah, containing the first five books of the Bible, is carried on the right arm by either the rabbi or another member of the congregation to the reader's desk in front of the altar, shown toward the west, south, east and north, so that all may see the writing; and, then, after a word of greeting ("The Lord be with you") the reader touches with a prayer shawl (taleth) the section to be read in the Torah and says: "Blessed be the Lord who is blessed for all eternity. Blessed art thou, Lord our God, ruler of the universe, Thou hast chosen us from all peoples and given us thy Torah."

To the orthodox Jew, God's relation with His people is a contractual bond, a covenant. He who led the children of Israel out of the bondage of Egypt revealed His divine law to them on Mount Sinai, long before the sons of the covenant (in Hebrew: B'nai Brith), under the influence of the prophets, came to the clear monotheistic concept of the Creator of the universe which characterizes Judaism since the Babylonian captivity.

In view of the fact that the Canaanites, in what is today the Republic of Israel and the Kingdom of Jordan, had their own local gods, the baalim (masters), and their own forms of worship, including the practice of human sacrifice and sexual orgies, the Hebrews or Israelites, emerging from the desert with rather "puritanistic" habits of life, trying to subdue the native inhabitants of the "Land of Promise," also had to prove that Yahweh, their God, was superior to the baalim. Since Yahweh, who had already shown his strength in Egypt, ought to be acknowledged by Moabites, Philistines, and the other Canaanites, the idea of Israel's mission developed, of Israel's task to be "a light to the Gentiles." The Israelites declared themselves "the chosen people" out of whose midst a Messiah (Christ) will rise to bring Israel's mission to its final glorious fulfillment. Then all the nations will "ascend the mountain of the Lord" and, under world government with its seat in Zion, all mankind will live a peaceful, harmonious existence. "Yahweh will be king over all the earth."

It goes without saying that the idea of the "chosen people" has been copied by both daughter religions of Judaism, Christianity and Islam. To this day, Catholicism insists that outside the Church there is no salvation. Similarly, Islam claims to be the only true religion, chosen to spread the faith of Allah (God) as declared by His prophet Mohammed. As could be expected, the early Christians, in order to justify their separation from Judaism, while not denying that the Jews had been "chosen" by God, claimed that because of their rejection of Jesus as the Messiah (or Christ), God had rejected the Jews and assigned their former role to the Church instead. The followers of the Islam, in turn, considering the Hebrew patriarchs of the Old Testament, Moses, the prophets, as well as Jesus of Nazareth, as important forerunners of their faith, insisted that because Jews and Christians had rejected the teachings of Mohammed, God had rejected both and handed over their function to the "only true" faith, Islam. Orthodox Judaism answered both daughter religions with a note of sarcasm: "What kind of God is this who can make such mistakes that He first reveals His divine commands to the Jews, then corrects Himself, chooses the Christians as His foremost servants, again realizes that He acted in error and finally concludes a third covenant, this time with Mohammed and the Arabs?"

Spinoza had but a weary smile for all this fanaticism, intolerance, and self-righteousness. "Every man's true happiness and blessedness," he writes in the *Theologico-Political Treatise*, "consists solely in the enjoyment of what is good, not in the pride that he alone is enjoying it, to the exclusion of others. He who thinks himself the more blessed because he is enjoying benefits which others are not, or because he is more blessed or more fortunate than his fellows, is ignorant of true happiness and blessedness, and the joy which he feels is either childish or envious and malicious. For instance, a man's true happiness consists only in wisdom, and the knowledge of the truth, not at all in the fact that he is wiser than others, or that others lack such knowledge: such considerations do not increase his wisdom or true happiness.

"Whoever, therefore, rejoices for such reasons, rejoices in another's misfortune, and is, so far, malicious and bad, knowing neither true happiness nor the peace of the true life . . . When God tells Solomon (1 Kings iii. 12) that no one shall be as wise as he in time to come, it seems to be only a manner of expressing surpassing wisdom; it is little to be believed that God would have promised Solomon, for his greater happiness, that He would never endow anyone with so much wisdom in time to come; this would in no wise have increased Solomon's intellect, and the wise king would have given equal thanks to the Lord if everyone had been gifted with the same faculties . . . We can now easily understand what is meant by the election of God. For since no one can do anything save by the predetermined order of nature, that is by God's eternal ordinance and decree, it follows that no one can choose a plan of life for himself, or accomplish any work save by God's vocation choosing him for the work or the plan of life in question, rather than any other. Lastly, by fortune, I mean the ordinance of God in so far as it directs human life through external and unexpected means. With these preliminaries I return to my purpose of discovering the reason why the Hebrews were said to be elected by God before other nations, and with the demonstration I thus proceed. All objects of legitimate desire fall, generally speaking, under one of these three categories:—

1. The knowledge of these things through their primary causes.

2. The government of the passions, or the acquirement of the habit of virtue.

3. Secure and healthy life.

"The means which most directly conduce towards the first two of these ends, and which may be considered their proximate and efficient causes are contained in human nature itself, so that their acquisition hinges only on our own power, and on the laws of human nature. It may be concluded that these gifts are not peculiar to any nation, but have always been shared by the whole human race, unless, indeed, we would indulge the dream that nature formerly created men of different kinds. But the means which conduce to security and health are chiefly in external circumstance, and are called the gifts of fortune because they depend chiefly on objective causes of which we are ignorant; for a fool may be almost as liable to happiness or unhappiness as a wise man. Nevertheless, human management and watchfulness can greatly assist towards living in security and warding off the injuries of our fellow-men, and even of beasts. Reason and experience show no more certain means of attaining this object than the formation of a society with fixed laws, the occupation of a strip of territory, and the concentration of all forces, as it were, into one body, that is the social body."[24]

Here Spinoza touches on something which, in the heat of arguments, both philosophers and theologians have neglected to observe, namely, the relationship between religion and civilization. Surely, if we conceive of God as the constructive, life-giving power that governs the universe, religion, which means the service of God, must deal with the totality of human life, with man's place in the universe, irrespective of his race, color, nationality, class or religious faith. In this sense, it must be "universal." But God reveals Himself differently to different people. A few are Spinozas or Einsteins or Gandhis climbing to the heights of human knowledge and sound intuition. Others understand God in more primitive terms. Different ethnic groups praise God in different languages, in different symbols. People who live together under similar geographic conditions, who share common experiences, who have common aspirations for the future, develop a particular group personality which we may also call a civilization. Their form of government, their laws, their customs, their art, their scientific endeavors, their philosophical speculations, their religious life express their historical tradition. This is no acknowledgement of "racism." An individual taken at birth out of the group into which he was born and reared in another group will undoubtedly identify himself with the civilization and culture of the second group. By the same token, an individual who derives no value from the group into which he was born, who believes that he might find self-realization in another group, should have the right to change his group allegiance or, if he is strong enough, live alone. But there have been, throughout the history of the human race, different human groups with their dis-

[24] *Ibid.*, Vol. I, pp. 43-46.

tinct group personality or civilization; and each group translates the meaning of God into its particular vocabulary.

The fifth commandment, "Kabed et awiha w'et imcha," (Honor thy father and thy mother,) is followed in the original Hebrew text by the words "l'maan yaarihun yameha al haadama asher Adonaj eloheha naten lah." (That thy days may be long upon the land which the Lord thy God gives thee.) Obviously, this whole commandment becomes meaningless unless each individual applies it to his own parents. It would be absurd to assume that each of us has the same responsibility toward the parents of others as he has toward his own parents. Yet, and this shows the interrelationship between the individual, his group, and the whole of humanity, the more we respect our own parents, our own elders, our own traditions, the more likely we are to respect the parents, the elders, the traditions of others.

Judaism, Spinoza realized, has its own ways of salvation, based on its historic tradition from the patriarchs, the exodus from Egypt, and the kingdoms of Juda and Israel to the restoration of the third Jewish commonwealth in our own day. In fact, it was rather easy for Spinoza to predict some 300 years ago that the Jews, in line with their civilization, would some day want to rebuild their national and cultural center in the "land of promise." Hinduism in India considers itself a civilization. So does Confucianism in China. So does Buddhism, the revolt against Brahman formalism. Islam and Christianity consider themselves "universal" religions. Yet it can be easily shown how deeply rooted both are in the cultural milieu of the peoples in whose midst these religions originated.

Islam, in doctrines and customs, is identified with the Arabs of the Arabian peninsula. When after the 7th century the Arabs overran Palestine, Syria, Iraq, and the North African coast, they imposed on the conquered populations the autocratic regime with which they were familiar; and to this day, the various units of the Moslem world, with the exception of non-Arab Turkey which under Ataturk separated state and church, are ruled like sheikdoms in the oases of Arabia.

Christianity is a direct outgrowth of Western civilization. It came into being as the result of a proselytizing movement in Judaism, deriving its impetus from the Messianic idea of the Jewish people, and the contact which this movement, under the leadership of Paul of Tarsus, made with the Greco-Roman world. Alexander's wars, followed by Roman imperialism, had caused the break-up of many local civilizations and their pagan cults. If Pax Romana was to become a reality, a religion was needed which could unify all the ethnic groups of the Roman Empire. The Stoa, forerunner of Christianity, supplied such a common ideology, but appealed only to the philosophically trained intellectuals of the time. Emperor worship, tried by the oriental empires and by Alexander of Macedonia, was doomed to failure largely because of the adamant opposition of the Jews, who, as Seneca testifies, exerted a noticeable influence in Rome.

During the life time of Jesus, Christianity was but a Jewish missionary sect. It became a separate religion only after Paul, conscious of the doctrines of the resurrected savior-gods in the mystery religions of Asia Minor, decided that his task was to convert the world to the idea that the man who was Jesus of Nazareth on earth, by his resurrection had been transformed into the divine redeemer. While the Jews rejected the Pauline conception of God, emphasizing God's oneness, the idea of the "only begotten Son of God" (John 3:16) appealed particularly to the

Greek pagans who, realizing the downfall of their culture, eagerly turned toward a faith which offered personal salvation and based it upon a divine redemptive act. Thanks to its Greek converts, Christianity rose from a small Jewish underground movement to its place as the official state religion of the Roman Empire. The very legend of how Emperor Constantine saw in his dream a cross and heard a voice proclaiming: "In hoc signo vinces," (in this sign you will conquer) demonstrates the significance of the Christian Church as the religious arm of Roman imperial power.

Throughout the Middle Ages, the idea of the Holy Roman Empire allowed the Bishop of Rome, because of his special position at the capital, to assume the role of the "pontifex maximus," the chief priest of pre-Christian Rome, and to become as pope the imperial head of an ecclesiastical hierarchy embracing all of Western Christianity. To this day, the language of Rome is the holy prayer tongue used in all Catholic churches, just as Hebrew is the prayer language of the Jews, and just as the Koran is recited in Arabic.

The close involvement of Christianity in the European civilization is, again, revealed by the Treaty of Westphalia, which, ending the Thirty Years' War in 1648, resolved its religious issue on the basis of "cuius regio eius religio" (the religion of the sovereign prince is to be the religion of the state). When Martin Luther, in October, 1517, posted his 95 theses on the church door at Wittenberg, he probably did not know that this act would complete the dissolution of the Holy Roman Empire and hasten the proliferation of independent national states in Europe. Nevertheless, the Protestant revolt was not only a matter of religious doctrine and a challenge to the supremacy of the papacy; it was also related to the struggle for emancipation of the national cultures of Northern Europe and to the desire of the European Kings and princes to establish their supreme legal and political power by severing their ties with Rome and "Romanism."

All monotheistic religions may claim catholicity in the sense that they try to serve the interests of all mankind and that their goal is the universal brotherhood of man. But neither Judaism nor Islam nor Christendom can lay claim to catholicity in the sense of being the one and only religion that is accepted by all or most of mankind. Like the non-monotheistic faiths, they are the religious expressions of particular civilizations; and to the extent to which they try to supplant other religions by coercive means, they can well be accused of "religious imperialism."

To Spinoza a faith does not demand that dogmas "should be true as that they should be pious. . . . As no one will dispute that men's dispositions are exceedingly varied, that all do not acquiesce in the same things, but are ruled some by one opinion some by another, so that what moves one to devotion moves another to laughter and contempt, it follows that there can be no doctrines in the Catholic, or universal, religion, which can give rise to controversy among good men. Such doctrines might be pious to some and impious to others, whereas they should be judged solely by their fruits.

"To the universal religion, then, belong only such dogmas as are absolutely required in order to attain obedience to God, and without which such obedience would be impossible; as for the rest, each man—seeing that he is the best judge of his own character—should adopt whatever he thinks best adapted to strengthen his love of justice. If this were so, I think there would be no further occasion for controversies in the Church."[25]

[25] *Ibid.*, Vol. I, pp. 185-186.

What Spinoza calls "universal faith" implies that no civilization, and therefore, no religion, has a copyright on its ideas and practices. While we may be loyal to our own civilization and to its religious expression without claiming that it alone affords salvation, we may very well assimilate useful ideas and practices of others to our own. No tradition is static; and there is no more danger of losing it by the adoption of other culture traits than there is that an individual will lose his individuality by borrowing from other individuals. If there is unity in God, an axiom which all great religions share, it must mean that all human beings and all human groups are objects of God's concern. Spinoza, therefore, insists that the religions, which in his days were largely a divisive force engendering animosities among human beings, should give up the notion of their "chosenness," their "election," their monopoly on salvation and unify the human race on the basis of those doctrines which are common to all of them.

These, according to Spinoza, are the doctrines common to all great religions:

"I. That God or a Supreme Being exists, sovereignly just and merciful, the Exemplar of the true life; that whosoever is ignorant of or disbelieves in His existence cannot obey Him or know Him as a Judge.

II. That He is One. Nobody will dispute that this doctrine is absolutely necessary for entire devotion, admiration, and love towards God. For devotion, admiration, and love spring from the superiority of one over all else.

III. That He is omnipresent, or that all things are open to Him, for if anything could be supposed to be concealed from Him, or to be unnoticed by Him, we might doubt or be ignorant of the equity of His judgement as directing all things.

IV. That He has supreme right and dominion over all

things, and that He does nothing under compulsion, but by His absolute fiat and grace. All things are bound to obey Him, He is not bound to obey any.

V. That the worship of God consists only in justice and charity, or love towards one's neighbour.

VI. That all those, and those only, who obey God by their manner of life are saved; the rest of mankind, who live under the sway of their pleasures, are lost. If we did not believe this, there would be no reason for obeying God rather than pleasure.

VII. Lastly, that God forgives the sins of those who repent. No one is free from sin, so that without this belief all would despair of salvation, and there would be no reason for believing in the mercy of God. He who firmly believes that God, out of the mercy and grace with which He directs all things, forgives the sins of men, and who feels his love of God kindled thereby, he, I say, does really know Christ according to the Spirit,[26] and Christ is in him.

"No one can deny that all these doctrines are before all things necessary to be believed, in order that every man, without exception, may be able to obey God according to the bidding of the Law above explained, for if one of these precepts be disregarded obedience is destroyed. But as to what God, or the Exemplar of the true life, may be, whether fire, or spirit, or light, or thought, or what not, this, I say, has nothing to do with faith any more than has the question how He comes to be the Exemplar of the true life, whether it be because He has a just and merciful mind, or because all things exist and act through Him, and consequently that we understand through Him, and

---

[26] In a letter to Oldenburg (Auerbach, Vol. II, p. 298) Spinoza says: "I am of the opinion that the resurrection of Christ from the dead was in truth a spiritual one which was revealed to the faithful in accordance with their capacity to understand such things." (My translation.)

through Him see what is truly just and good. Everyone may think on such questions as he likes.

"Furthermore, faith is not affected, whether we hold that God is omnipresent essentially or potentially; that He directs all things by absolute fiat, or by the necessity of His nature; that He dictates laws like a prince, or that He sets them forth as eternal truths; that man obeys Him by virtue of free will, or by virtue of the necessity of the Divine decree; lastly, that the reward of the good and the punishment of the wicked is natural or supernatural: these and such like questions have no bearing on faith, except in so far as they are used as means to give us license to sin more, or to obey God less. I will go further, and maintain that every man is bound to adapt these dogmas to his own way of thinking, and to interpret them according as he feels that he can give them his fullest and most unhesitating assent, so that he may the more easily obey God with his whole heart."[27]

Thinking in terms of the unity of God and mankind, Spinoza, though reared in the Jewish tradition and loyal to its fundamental tenets, had no difficulty in accepting the personality of Jesus of Nazareth as one of the most outstanding representatives of "universal faith." Jesus was in the best of the Jewish prophetic tradition. He never thought of himself as anything but a Jew, and he expressly told his followers in Judea, "Think not that I am come to destroy the law or the Prophets. I am not come to destroy but to fulfill. For verily I say unto you, till heaven and earth pass, one jot or one tittle shall in nowise pass from the Law, till all be fulfilled. Whosoever, therefore, shall break one of the least commandments, and shall teach men so, he shall be called the least in the Kingdom of Heaven." (Matthew 5:17-19.)

[27] *Ibid.*, Vol. I, pp. 186-188.

It is true, there are instances recorded in the New Testament according to which Jesus and his disciples did not observe some of the ceremonials which the Pharisees cherished. But as the whole of the Talmudic literature shows, the Pharisees, too, did not agree on all matters of ritual. In fact, liberal Judaism in our day has done away with much of the ceremonial detail without committing itself to any new religious values. To a man like Spinoza, Jesus' "Sermon on the Mount" must have had a particular appeal, though even he, who certainly did not practice revenge, rejected the principle of non-resistance as an invitation to aggression. Neither Spinoza nor any liberal Jew could agree with Jesus' attitude toward the Gentiles, expressed in his admonition to his disciples: "Go not into the way of the Gentiles, and into any city of the Samaritans[28] enter ye not. But go rather to the lost sheep of the house of Israel." (Matthew 10:5-6). If anything, these words show that it was Paul, not Jesus, who thought in terms of a new religion no longer rooted in Jewish civilization and, therefore, more acceptable to the pagan converts of Greece and Rome. Neither Spinoza nor any liberal thinker could accept the mission of Jesus described in Matthew (10:34-35): "Think not that I am come to send peace on earth: I come not to send peace, but a sword. For I am come to set a man at variance against his father, and the daughter against her mother, and the daughter in law against her mother in law." Indeed, these words sound like a complete departure from Jesus' other teachings and are probably quoted out of context. At any rate, they could easily form the basis of religious persecution which would not be conducive to "universal faith."

When asked what his first commandment was, Jesus answered in the words of the two most fundamental

---

[28] A Jewish sect outside of the mainstream of Judaism.

Jewish prayers, taken from Deuteronomy: "The first of all the commandments is, Hear, O Israel; The Lord our God is one Lord. And thou shalt love the Lord thy God with all thy heart, and with all thy soul, and with all thy mind and with all thy strength. This is the first commandment." (Mark 12:29-30) As the second in importance Jesus quotes Leviticus (19:18) "Thou shalt love thy neighbor as thyself," adding the words of Hillel, "there is none other commandment greater than these." (Mark 12:31)

Claude Montefiore, the great English Jewish scholar, was probably quite right in saying:

"Yet the time will surely come when the roll of Israel's prophets will be acknowledged by Jews themselves not to close before the prophet of Nazareth . . . Modern Judaism needs both the rabbis and Jesus . . . Both are bone of the Jewish bone, and spirit of the Jewish spirit."[29]

This is not the place to analyze why the Jews have not accepted Jesus as the Messiah and why even in our time so relatively few Jews have found it possible to present an unbiased picture of the remarkable role which the Nazarene has played in the development of Judeo-Christianity and the whole of Western thought.[30] Spinoza, to whom theological rancor was foreign and who did not feel the need of replying in kind to the epithet "Christ Killer" with which non-Jewish demagogues and ignoramuses taunt Jews, recognized that, in spite of different civilizational backgrounds, Judaism and Christendom are one in their love of God and in their belief in the brotherhood of man. He knew that the "voice of God" is more often than not the voice of a human animal, invoking the Deity

[29] Claude G. Montefiore, *The Snyoptic Gospels*, London, 1909, Vol. II., p. 1098.
[30] Such an analysis I have attempted in *The Republic of Israel*, New York, 1950, Chap. 1.

to gain respect for his ideas and wishes, however asocial and unholy they may be. But this did not prevent Spinoza from setting up a goal of conscious God-relatedness for the human race. For he realized that, while man should have the right to earn his bread, he "cannot live by bread alone."

Spinoza's Political Thought

BY THE END of the seventeenth century, the rise of national monarchies and the growth of urban industries had destroyed the medieval ideal of feudalism and European unity under the sway of the Roman papacy. The landed aristocracy and the clergy were losing their political importance to the princes and city burghers, who, in turn, fought the struggle for either royal or popular sovereignty within the new framework of the national states, accompanied on the world scene by international rivalries in commerce, diplomacy and warfare. Roman law and the Justinian dictum that the king's will has legal force, combined with economic and fiscal needs, helped the kings of England, Spain and France, at least temporarily, to establish royal despotism. On the other hand, the accumulation of wealth by the new class of merchants and manufacturers, demanding participation in the government of their countries, served as a check against absolutism.

In the Netherlands, the persecution of the Protestants by Catholic Spain, together with the Spanish interference in local government and the levying of financial burdens on the entire populace, had led to the revolt of the northern provinces and their establishment as an independent republic. The success of this revolt was particularly conducive to political thought. For, in their attempt to justify their national independence and freedom from Spanish rule, the intellectual leaders of the Netherlands collected all the arguments which were needed to answer those who either idealized absolute monarchy or pleaded for the unlimited temporal authority of the papacy.

Anti-monarchic doctrines of social contract and of the laws of nature, interpreted through human reason and the dictates of conscience, principles of religious tolerance, the concept of the rule of law in international relations, and the equality of all states in international law, i.e. mainly European and later American law, all these became a formidable arsenal of thought in the Dutch struggle against the Spanish monarchy as well as in the English contest with Louis XIV of France.

While the great Dutch jurist Hugo Grotius, in *De Jure Belli ac Pacis* (published in 1625), developed the modern principles of international law, it was Spinoza, who, aiming to secure freedom of thought and of expression for all the members of the state, established the doctrines of the common or general will of the people, of human equality, and of popular sovereignty.[1] Had he lived longer, it would have become quite clear that Spinoza's major interest was not at all in metaphysics, but rather in the development of a modern political science. Because of *The Ethics* and its philosophical speculations, the name of Spinoza is usually attached to terms like "mysticism" and "pantheism," rather than to "freedom of thought" and "democracy." School philosophers who consider it a defect in Spinoza's system of philosophy that it takes but little notice of epistemology, do not realize that Spinoza did not consider it his task to theorize on the possibility of a subject knowing an object, but rather pondered about the problem of evolving a rational political ethic for modern

[1] While Rousseau plagiarized Spinoza's basic concepts, John Locke developed similar concepts along independent lines of thought for the British scene.

life and the need to replace super-natural sanctions for social conduct by God-given human reason.

Spinoza shares with Hobbes a common fund of terminology. Natural and civil right, state of nature, the compact with which the state comes into being—these and other expressions suggest a kindred approach to political phenomena. But in their interpretation of these rather ambiguous terms and in their political direction and ethics, the two men have very little in common.

Hobbes, long before Karl Marx, is the materialist *par excellence* and at the same time the most outspoken protagonist of the absolutist theory of the state. Living in the midst of political turmoil which offended his longing for geometrical order, he dwells on the fallibility of human nature, on the chaos which it produces, and the perpetual war of every man against his neighbor in the state of nature, i.e. in pre-political human existence. Confronted with the alternatives of relying solely upon his own power to destroy his fellow man (and be destroyed by him) or a social compact in which man contracts with every other man to surrender his liberty of using his own power in order to achieve mutual security, the human race, according to Hobbes, created that great Leviathan, the State.

"He (the Leviathan or State) hath the use of so much Power and Strength conferred on him, that by terror thereof, he is inabled to forme the wills of them all . . . And in him consisteth the Essence of the Commonwealth; which is One Person, of whose Acts a great Multitude, by mutuall Covenants one with another, have made themselves every one the Author, to the end he may use the strength and means of them all, as he shall think expedient, for their Peace and Common Defence . . . And he that carryeth this Person, is called Soveraigne, and said to have Soveraigne Power; and every one besides, his subject."[2]

Spinoza knew as well as Hobbes the dangers of anarchy in an undisciplined democracy. "The fickle disposition of the multitude," he writes, "almost reduces those who have experience of it to despair, for it is governed solely by emotions, not by reason: it rushes head-long into every enterprise, and is easily corrupted either by avarice or luxury: everyone thinks himself omniscient and wishes to fashion all things to his liking, judging a thing to be just or unjust, lawful or unlawful, according as he thinks it will bring him profit or loss: vanity leads him to despise his equals, and refuse their guidance: envy of superior fame or fortune (for such gifts are never equally distributed) leads him to desire and rejoice in his neighbour's downfall. I need not go through the whole list, everyone knows how much crime results from disgust at the present —desire for change, headlong anger, and contempt for poverty—and how men's minds are engrossed and kept in turmoil thereby."[3]

But unlike Hobbes, who dreaded his fellowmen, undoubtedly because of his own unanalyzed aggressiveness, Spinoza never lost his almost boundless compassion with all human beings. In a rare moment of generosity, Nietzsche, probably better than anyone else, characterized Spinoza's personality in these words: "Spinoza deified the All in order to find peace and happiness in the face of it. . . ."[4]

Spinoza agreed with Hobbes that self-interest or self-preservation is the chief motive of human action. "Now it is the sovereign law and right of nature that each indi-

---

[2] Hobbes, *Leviathan*, Everyman's Library, 1914, pp. 89-90.
[3] Spinoza, *op. cit.*, Vol. I., pp. 216-217.
[4] Nietzsche, *Der Willezur Macht*, § 95. (My translation.)

vidual should endeavour to preserve itself as it is, without regard to anything but itself; therefore this sovereign law and right belongs to every individual, namely, to exist and act according to its natural conditions. We do not here acknowledge any difference between mankind and other individual natural entities, nor between men endowed with reason and those to whom reason is unknown; nor between fools, madmen, and sane men. Whatsoever an individual does by the laws of its nature it has a sovereign right to do, inasmuch as it acts as it was conditioned by nature, and cannot act otherwise. Wherefore among men, so long as they are considered as living under the sway of nature, he who does not yet know reason, or who has not yet acquired the habit of virtue, acts solely according to the laws of his desire with as sovereign a right as he who orders his life entirely by the laws of reason.

"That is, as the wise man has sovereign right to do all that reason dictates, or to live according to the laws of reason, so also the ignorant and foolish man has sovereign right to do all that desire dictates, or to live according to the laws of desire. This is identical with the teaching of Paul, who acknowledges that previous to the law—that is, so long as men are considered of as living under the sway of nature, there is no sin.

"The natural right of the individual man is thus determined, not by sound reason, but by desire and power. All are not naturally conditioned so as to act according to the laws and rules of reason; nay, on the contrary, all men are born ignorant, and before they can learn the right way of life and acquire the habit of virtue, the greater part of their life, even if they have been well brought up, has passed away. Nevertheless, they are in the meanwhile bound to live and preserve themselves as far as they can by the unaided impulses of desire. Nature has given them no other guide, and has denied them the present power of living according to sound reason; so that they are no more bound to live by the dictates of an enlightened mind, than a cat is bound to live by the laws of the nature of a lion."[5]

Was there a pre-political state of nature, brutish and bestial, as Hobbes thought it was, or was it "a state of liberty" under the reign of law, which prescribed equality and reason, as John Locke conceived of it?[6] Spinoza saw no valid justification in bothering with such romantic myths and fictions. He realized that there is an acute social problem because men are not "naturally" social-minded, i.e. altruistic. Men are political animals. They show social tendencies; but born in ignorance, they have to be trained to live in society. Meanwhile, as children demonstrate, they preserve themselves as best they can by impulse. They may fight, hate, exploit and cheat until experience and reason give them a "conscience," a sense of what is "right" and "wrong," a "superego" which internalizes the demands made by society on the individual.

Given the normal development of intelligence and constructive social thought, the discordant strife of human personalities might yield to social cooperation and harmony. "When we reflect that men without mutual help, or the aid of reason, must needs live most miserably, as we clearly proved in Chap. V., we shall plainly see that men must necessarily come to an agreement to live together as securely and well as possible if they are to enjoy as a whole the rights which naturally belong to them as individuals, and their life should be no more conditioned by the force and desire of individuals, but by the power

[5] *Ibid.*, Vol. I, pp. 200-201.
[6] John Locke, *Two Treatises of Civil Government,* Everyman's Library, 1924, pp. 118-120.

and will of the whole body. This end they will be unable to attain if desire be their only guide (for by the laws of desire each man is drawn in a different direction); they must, therefore, most firmly decree and establish that they will be guided in everything by reason (which nobody will dare openly to repudiate lest he should be taken for a madman), and will restrain any desire which is injurious to a man's fellows, that they will do to all as they would be done by, and that they will defend their neighbour's rights as their own."[7]

Under the tyranny of impulse, there is fear and greed. But the inner source of man's strength is that he has the capacity to realize his weakness. "Now it is a universal law of human nature that no one ever neglects anything which he judges to be good, except with the hope of gaining a greater good, or from the fear of a greater evil; nor does anyone endure an evil except for the sake of avoiding a greater evil, or gaining a greater good. That is, everyone will, of two goods, choose that which he thinks the greatest; and, of two evils, that which he thinks the least. I say advisedly that which he thinks the greatest or the least, for it does not necessarily follow that he judges right. This law is so deeply implanted in the human mind that it ought to be counted among eternal truths and axioms.

"As a necessary consequence of the principle just enunciated, no one can honestly promise to forego the right which he has over all things, and in general no one will abide by his promises, unless under the fear of a greater evil, or the hope of a greater good. An example will make the matter clearer. Suppose that a robber forces me to promise that I will give him my goods at his will and pleasure. It is plain (inasmuch as my natural right is, as

[7] Spinoza, *op. cit,* Vol. I, pp. 202-203.

I have shown, co-extensive with my power) that if I can free myself from this robber by stratagem, by assenting to his demands, I have the natural right to do so, and to pretend to accept his conditions. Or, again, suppose I have genuinely promised someone that for the space of twenty days I will not taste food or any nourishment; and suppose I afterwards find that my promise was foolish, and cannot be kept without very great injury to myself; as I am bound by natural law and right to choose the least of two evils, I have complete right to break my compact, and act as if my promise had never been uttered. I say that I should have perfect natural right to do so, whether I was actuated by true and evident reason, or whether I was actuated by mere opinion in thinking I had promised rashly; whether my reasons were true or false, I should be in fear of a greater evil, which, by the ordinance of nature, I should strive to avoid by every means in my power.

"We may, therefore, conclude that a compact is only made valid by its utility, without which it becomes null and void. It is therefore, foolish to ask a man to keep his faith with us for ever, unless we also endeavour that the violation of the compact we enter into shall involve for the violator more harm than good. This consideration should have very great weight in forming a state. However, if all men could be easily led by reason alone, and could recognize what is best and most useful for a state, there would be no one who would not forswear deceit, for everyone would keep most religiously to their compact in their desire for the chief good, namely, the preservation of the state, and would cherish good faith above all things as the shield and buckler of the commonwealth. However, it is far from being the case that all men can always be easily led by reason alone; everyone is drawn away by his pleasure, while avarice, ambition, envy, hatred, and the like so engross the mind that reason has no place therein. Hence, though men make promises with all the appearances of good faith, and agree that they will keep to their engagement, no one can absolutely rely on another man's promise unless there is something behind it. Everyone has by nature a right to act deceitfully, and to break his compacts, unless he be restrained by the hope of some greater good, or the fear of some greater evil."[8]

This is obviously not the Hobbesian social contract for the establishment of the Leviathan-state, nor is it the Lockeian concept of the *laissez faire, laissez aller*, night watchman state. Spinoza realized the fallacy of the social contract theory in both its historical and its logical aspects. He knew that states were often organized by conquest or usurpation and that in most parts of the earth obedience was rendered to the state because of the habitual conditioning of the people, rather than because of any original contract. Moreover, if such a contract did exist, it could not bind the descendants of the original contractors anyhow.

While unlike Locke, he had little faith in any absolute goodness of human nature, he also rejected the idea of an absolute wickedness which Hobbes ascribed to the human animal. According to Spinoza, man's capacity for reasoning and for a fuller life grows in his interrelationship with other human beings, and the basis of authority is its obvious utility for man in social life. While Hobbes believes that man had "natural rights" before entering the state and that whatever "natural rights" he retained, are retained by him apart from the state, Spinoza holds that all rights must flow from the consciousness of a common interest on the part of all citizens of the state.

[8] *Ibid.*, Vol. I, pp. 203-204.

In contrast to Jeremy Bentham, who leads the utilitarian concept ad absurdum by attempting a sort of mathematical computation of individual pains and pleasures, the "felicific calculus," as some commentators dubbed the guiding idea of his writings, Spinoza, always aware of man's social tendencies, tries to bridge the chasm between individual and community satisfactions. To him, the task of intelligent statecraft is to understand the nature of power and to utilize it for the enhancement and the maturing of the individuals who form the community. And while he seeks the path of moral, God-related and therefore man-related life under any form of government, he believes that a representative democracy would, in the long run, be most consistent with his concept of utility.

"A body politic of this kind," he writes, "is called a Democracy, which may be defined as a society which wields all its power as a whole. The sovereign power is not restrained by any laws, but everyone is bound to obey it in all things; such is the state of things implied when men either tacitly or expressly handed over to it all their power of self-defence, or in other words, all their right. For if they had wished to retain any right for themselves, they ought to have taken precautions for its defence and preservation; as they have not done so, and indeed could not have done so without dividing and consequently ruining the state, they placed themselves absolutely at the mercy of the sovereign power; and, therefore, having acted (as we have shown) as reason and necessity demanded, they are obliged to fulfill the commands of the sovereign power, however absurd these may be, else they will be public enemies, and will act against reason, which urges the preservation of the state as a primary duty. For reason bids us choose the least of two evils.

"Furthermore, this danger of submitting absolutely to

the domination and will of another, is one which may be incurred with a light heart: for we have shown that sovereigns only possess this right of imposing their will, so long as they have the full power to enforce it: if such power be lost their right to command is lost also, or lapses to those who have assumed it and can keep it. Thus it is very rare for sovereigns to impose thoroughly irrational commands, for they are bound to consult their own interests, and retain their power by consulting the public good and acting according to the dictates of reason, as Seneca says, violenta imperia nemo continuit diu. No one can long retain a tyrant's sway.

"In a democracy, irrational commands are still less to be feared: for it is almost impossible that the majority of a people, especially if it be a large one, should agree in an irrational design: and, moreover, the basis and aim of a democracy is to avoid the desires as irrational, and to bring men as far as possible under the control of reason, so that they may live in peace and harmony: if this basis be removed the whole fabric falls to ruin."[9]

Unlike his forerunners and contemporaries, Spinoza clearly separates state and government. Dictatorship he rules out of court. "That commonwealth," he writes in the *Political Treatise,* "whose peace depends on the sluggishness of its subjects, that are led about like sheep, to learn but slavery, may more properly be called a desert than a commonwealth."[10]

Monarchy, in the sense that one man actually exercises sovereign power, he considers indefensible in theory and unsound in practice. "For no man is so watchful, that he never falls asleep; and no man ever had a character so vigorous and honest, but he sometimes, and that just

[9] *Ibid.,* Vol. I, pp. 205-206.
[10] *Ibid.,* Vol. I, p. 314.

when strength of character was most wanted, was diverted from his purpose and let himself be overcome. And it is surely folly to require of another what one can never obtain from one's self; I mean, that he should be more watchful for another's interest than his own, that he should be free from avarice, envy, and ambition, and so on; especially when he is one, who is subject daily to the strongest temptations of every passion.

"But, on the other hand, experience is thought to teach, that it makes for peace and concord, to confer the whole authority upon one man. For no dominion has stood so long without any notable change, as that of the Turks, and on the other hand there were none so little lasting, as those, which were popular or democratic, nor any in which so many seditions arose. Yet if slavery, barbarism, and desolation are to be called peace, men can have no worse misfortune. No doubt there are usually more and sharper quarrels between parents and children, than between masters and slaves; yet it advances not the art of housekeeping, to change a father's right into a right of property, and count children but as slaves. Slavery then, not peace, is furthered by handing over to one man the whole authority. For peace, as we said before, consists not in mere absence of war, but in a union or agreement of minds.

"And in fact they are much mistaken, who suppose that one man can by himself hold the supreme right of a commonwealth. For the only limit of right, as we showed (Chap. II.), is power. But the power of one man is very inadequate to support so great a load. And hence it arises, that the man, whom the multitude had chosen king, seeks out for himself generals, or counsellors, or friends, to whom he entrusts his own and the common welfare; so that the dominion, which is thought to be a perfect monarchy, is in actual working an aristocracy, not, indeed, an open but a hidden one, and therefore the worst of all. Besides which a king, who is a boy, or ill, or overcome by age, is but king on sufferance; and those in this case have the supreme authority, who administer the highest business of the dominion, or are near the king's person; not to mention, that a lascivious king often manages everything at the caprice of this or that mistress or minion."[11]

Some textbook writers insist that Spinoza followed "machiavellian" precepts in his design for the most successful organization of the state. If we remember Machiavelli's biting criticism of Savonarola's opportunism[12] and his *Discourses on Livy,* the author of *The Prince* will appear to be far less "machiavellian" than is generally assumed. Indeed, as Spinoza alludes, we cannot be at all sure whether *The Prince* was not written to warn against despotic government rather than to advocate it.

Anyway, here is the full quotation from Spinoza on Machiavelli in the *Political Treatise.* The reader may judge for himself whether Spinoza follows Machiavelli in the customary "machiavellian" vein attributed to the great political scientist of the Renaissance. "But what means a prince, whose sole motive is lust of mastery, should use to establish and maintain his dominion, the most ingenious Machiavelli has set forth at large, but with what design one can hardly be sure. If, however, he had some good design, as one should believe of a learned man, it seems to have been to show, with how little foresight many attempt to remove a tyrant, who can in no wise be removed, but, on the contrary, is so much the more established, as the prince is given more cause to fear, which happens when the multitude has made an example

[11] *Ibid.,* Vol. I, pp. 317-318.
[12] Nicolo Machiavelli, *Lettere,* Firence, 1929, p. 5.

of its prince, and glories in the parricide as in a thing well done. Moreover, he perhaps wished to show how cautious a free multitude should be of entrusting its welfare absolutely to one man, who, unless in his vanity he thinks he can please everybody, must be in daily fear of plots, and so is forced to look chiefly after his own interests, and, as for the multitude, rather to plot against it than consult its good. And I am the more led to this opinion concerning that most farseeing man, because it is known that he was favourable to liberty, for the maintenance of which he has besides given the most wholesome advice."[13]

It has also been said that Spinoza leaned toward an aristocratic republic, and his detailed treatment "Of Aristocracy" in the *Political Treatise* might lend some justification to this notion. But it must be emphasized that the "constitution" of which he speaks in his chapters on aristocratic government does not exclude the common citizens from affairs of government. "And what we have written will, perhaps, be received with derision by those who limit to the populace only the vices which are inherent in all mortals; and use such phrases as, the mob, if it is not frightened, inspires no little fear, and the populace is either a humble slave, or a haughty master, and it has no truth or judgment, etc. But all have one common nature. Only we are deceived by power and refinement. Whence it comes that when two do the same thing we say, this man may do it with impunity, that man may not; not because the deed, but because the doer is different. Haughtiness is a property of rulers. Men are haughty, but by reason of an appointment for a year; how much more then nobles, that have their honours eternal! But their arrogance is glossed over with importance, luxury, pro-

---

[13] Spinoza, *op. cit.*, Vol. I, p. 315.

fusion, and a kind of harmony of vices, and a certain cultivated folly, and elegant villainy, so that vices, each of which looked at separately is foul and vile, because it is then most conspicuous, appear to the inexperienced and untaught honourable and becoming. The mob, too, if it is not frightened, inspires no little fear; yes, for liberty and slavery are not easily mingled. Lastly, as for the populace being devoid of truth and judgment, that is nothing wonderful, since the chief business of the dominion is transacted behind its back, and it can but make conjectures from the little, which cannot be hidden. For it is an uncommon virtue to suspend one's judgment. So it is supreme folly to wish to transact everything behind the backs of the citizens, and to expect that they will not judge ill of the same, and will not give everything an unfavourable interpretation. For if the populace could moderate itself, and suspend its judgment about things with which it is imperfectly acquainted, or judge rightly of things by the little it knows already, it would surely be more fit to govern, than to be governed."[14]

The last chapter of the *Political Treatise,* entitled "Of Democracy," remained a fragment. While Spinoza states that the type of democracy which favors those who happen to be rich (i.e., an oligarchy) might be considered inferior to an aristocracy, there is no indication in his plan for the chapter that he would not prefer democracy, based on equality of opportunity, to aristocratic government. These are his words:

"I pass, at length, to the third and perfectly absolute dominion, which we call democracy. The difference between this and aristocracy consists, we have said, chiefly in this, that in an aristocracy it depends on the supreme council's will and free choice only, that this or that man

[14] *Ibid.,* Vol. I, pp. 340-341.

is made a patrician, so that no one has the right to vote or fill public offices by inheritance, and that no one can by right demand this right, as is the case in the dominion, whereof we are now treating. For all, who are born of citizen parents, or on the soil of the country, or who have deserved well of the republic, or have accomplished any other conditions upon which the law grants to a man right of citizenship; they all, I say, have a right to demand for themselves the right to vote in the supreme council and to fill public offices, nor can they be refused it, but for crime or infamy.

"If then, it is by a law appointed, that the elder men only, who have reached a certain year of their age, or the first-born only, as soon as their age allows, or those who contribute to the republic a certain sum of money, shall have the right of voting in the supreme council and managing the business of the dominion; then, although on this system the result might be, that the supreme council would be composed of fewer citizens than that of the aristocracy of which we treated above, yet, for all that, dominions of this kind should be called democracies, because in them the citizens, who are destined to manage affairs of state, are not chosen as the best by the supreme council, but are destined to it by a law. And although for this reason dominions of this kind, that is, where not the best, but those who happen by chance to be rich, or who are born eldest, are destined to govern, are thought inferior to an aristocracy; yet, if we reflect on the practice or general condition of mankind, the result in both cases will come to the same thing. For patricians will always think those the best, who are rich, or related to themselves in blood, or allied by friendship. And, indeed, if such were the nature of patricians, that they were free from all passion, and guided by mere zeal for the public welfare in choosing their patrician colleagues, no dominion could be compared with aristocracy. But experience itself teaches us only too well, that things pass in quite a contrary manner, above all, in oligarchies, where the will of the patricians, from the absence of rivals, is most free from the law. For there the patricians intentionally keep away the best men from the council, and seek for themselves such colleagues in it, as hang upon their words, so that in such a dominion things are in a much more unhappy condition, because the choice of patricians depends entirely upon the arbitrary will of a few, which is free or unrestrained by any law. But I return to my subject.

"From what has been said in the last section, it is manifest that we can conceive of various kinds of democracy. But my intention is not to treat of every kind, but of that only, wherein all, without exception, who owe allegiance to the laws of the country only, and are further independent and of respectable life, have the right of voting in the supreme council and of filling the offices of the dominion. I say expressly, who owe allegiance to the laws of the country only, to exclude foreigners, who are treated as being under another's dominion. I added, besides, who are independent, except in so far as they are under the authority of parents and guardians. I said, lastly, and of respectable life, to exclude, above all, those that are infamous from crime, or some disgraceful means of livelihood . . ."[15]

Hobbes was concerned chiefly with establishing the absolute nature of sovereignty. Spinoza, on the contrary, was concerned with individual freedom, so that man could live in accordance with reason. But, the question arises, how can there be any individual freedom, any minority rights to stand against the general will, which, for the

[15] *Ibid.*, Vol. I, pp. 385-386.

greater good of all, must be obeyed by all? Spinoza answers this question by pointing out that the social compact must always remain in many respects purely ideal.

"No one can ever so utterly transfer to another his power and, consequently, his rights, as to cease to be a man; nor can there ever be a power so sovereign that it can carry out every possible wish. It will always be vain to order a subject to hate what he believes brings him advantage, or to love what brings him loss, or not to be offended at insults, or not to wish to be free from fear, or a hundred other things of the sort, which necessarily follow from the laws of human nature."[16]

No sovereign can or ought ever to control man's mind. Freedom of thought and of expression is not only essential to the individual citizen; it is just as important to the state, to society as a whole. We must have the possible profit of even the most dangerous heresy. If this sounds trite, let us remember that Spinoza wrote at a time when the famed Descartes was modifying his philosophy in order to pacify the Catholic church and when Galileo's retraction was still fresh in the memory of Europe's intellectuals. Let us also remember that freedom of thought and expression is by no means guaranteed in large parts of the world in which we live, and that there are forces at work in our own country which would gladly stifle this freedom in order to manipulate the masses of the people at will.

To Spinoza, laws against free speech were subversive of law itself and moreover, in the long run, futile. "If men's minds were as easily controlled as their tongues, every king would sit safely on his throne, and government by compulsion would cease; for every subject would shape his life according to the intentions of his rulers, and would

[16] *Ibid.*, Vol. I, p. 214.

esteem a thing true or false, good or evil, just or unjust, in obedience to their dictates. However, we have shown already (Chapter XVII.) that no man's mind can possibly lie wholly at the disposition of another, for no one can willingly transfer his natural right of free reason and judgment, or be compelled so to do. For this reason government which attempts to control minds is accounted tyrannical, and it is considered an abuse of sovereignty and a usurpation of the rights of subjects, to seek to prescribe what shall be accepted as true, or rejected as false, or what opinions should actuate men in their worship of God. All these questions fall within a man's natural right, which he cannot abdicate even with his own consent."[17]

Men who think will speak their thoughts in spite of prohibitions. The state may demand the right to control speech. But Spinoza doubts the wisdom of such a demand. This is the crucial point of both political treatises, the *Theologico-Political Treatise* and the *Political Treatise*:

"The ultimate aim of government is not to rule, or restrain, by fear, nor to exact obedience, but contrariwise, to free every man from fear, that he may live in all possible security; in other words, to strengthen his natural right to exist and work without injury to himself or others.

"No, the object of government is not to change men from rational beings into beasts or puppets, but to enable them to develop their minds and bodies in security, and to employ their reason unshackled; neither showing hatred, anger, or deceit, nor watched with the eyes of jealousy and injustice. In fact, the true aim of government is liberty."[18]

[17] *Ibid.*, Vol. I, p. 257.
[18] *Ibid.*, Vol. I, p. 259.

Freedom of speech makes for social vitality; and wherever a democracy is not just a facade, it will invite rather than curb freedom of speech. For, apart from demagogues and psychopaths, there are no citizens so loyal as those men and women who know that they may criticize their government with impunity as long as they do not indulge in slander.

Freedom of thought does not, however, imply freedom of action. Spinoza emphasizes this point. "For although men's free judgments are very diverse, each one thinking that he alone knows everything, and although complete unanimity of feeling and speech is out of the question, it is impossible to preserve peace, unless individuals abdicate their right of acting entirely on their own judgment. Therefore, the individual justly cedes the right of free action, though not of free reason and judgment; no one can act against the authorities without danger to the state, though his feelings and judgment may be at variance therewith; he may even speak against them, provided that he does so from rational conviction, not from fraud, anger, or hatred, and provided that he does not attempt to introduce any change on his private authority. For instance, supposing a man shows that a law is repugnant to sound reason, and should therefore be repealed; if he submits his opinion to the judgment of the authorities (who, alone, have the right of making and repealing laws), and meanwhile acts in nowise contrary to that law, he has deserved well of the state, and has behaved as a good citizen should; but if he accuses the authorities of injustice, and stirs up the people against them, or if he seditiously strives to abrogate the law without their consent, he is a mere agitator and rebel.

"Thus we see how an individual may declare and teach what he believes, without injury to the authority of his rulers, or to the public peace; namely, by leaving in their hands the entire power of legislation as it affects action, and by doing nothing against their laws, though he may be compelled often to act in contradiction to what he believes, and openly feels to be the best."[19]

Spinoza is aware of the possibility that thoughts and utterances cannot always be clearly separated from action. Those opinions "which by their very nature nullify the compact by which the right of free action was ceded"[20] must be considered as seditious.[21] But this admission is followed by a credo which many legislators, even in our free American democracy, will be wise to read and reread.

"If we hold to the principle that a man's loyalty to the state should be judged, like his loyalty to God, from his actions only—namely, from his charity towards his neighbours; we cannot doubt that the best government will allow freedom of philosophical speculation no less than of religious belief. I confess that from such freedom inconveniences may sometimes arise, but what question was ever settled so wisely that no abuses could possibly spring therefrom? He who seeks to regulate everything by law, is more likely to arouse vices than to reform them. It is best to grant what cannot be abolished, even though it be in itself harmful. How many evils spring from luxury, envy, avarice, drunkenness, and the like, yet these are tolerated—vices as they are—because they cannot be prevented by legal enactments. How much more then should free thought be granted, seeing that it is in itself a virtue and that it cannot be crushed! Besides, the evil results

[19] *Ibid.,* Vol. I, pp. 259-260.
[20] *Ibid.,* Vol. I, p. 260.
[21] Communists and Fascists who advocate the overthrow of democratic government and exploit maladjustments in social life to stage *coups d'état* with the aim of replacing individual rights by the terroristic dictate of either a communist or a fascist "élite", must therefore be classified as seditious elements.

can easily be checked, as I will show, by the secular authorities, not to mention that such freedom is absolutely necessary for progress in science and the liberal arts: for no man follows such pursuits to advantage unless his judgment be entirely free and unhampered.

"But let it be granted that freedom may be crushed, and men be so bound down, that they do not dare to utter a whisper, save at the bidding of their rulers; nevertheless this can never be carried to the pitch of making them think according to authority, so that the necessary consequences would be that men would daily be thinking one thing and saying another, to the corruption of good faith, that mainstay of government, and to the fostering of hateful flattery and perfidy, whence spring stratagems, and the corruption of every good art."[22]

The unfinished *Political Treatise,* planned as a comprehensive, critical textbook of political science in conjunction with the *Theologico-Political Treatise,* shows clearly that Spinoza was not inclined to ascribe to man virtues that he does not possess.

"Philosophers . . ." he writes, "think they are doing something wonderful, and reaching the pinnacle of learning, when they are clever enough to bestow manifold praise on such human nature, as is nowhere to be found, and to make verbal attacks on that which, in fact, exists. For they conceive of men, not as they are, but as they themselves would like them to be. Whence it has come to pass that, instead of ethics, they have generally written satire, and that they have never conceived a theory of politics, which could be turned to use, but such as might be taken for a chimera, or might have been formed in Utopia, or in that golden age of the poets when, to be sure, there was least need of it. Accordingly, as in all

[22] *Ibid.*, Vol. I, p. 261.

sciences, which have a useful application, so especially in that of politics, theory is supposed to be at variance with practice; and no men are esteemed less fit to direct public affairs than theorists or philosophers.

"But statesmen, on the other hand, are suspected of plotting against mankind, rather than consulting their interests, and are esteemed more crafty than learned. No doubt nature has taught them, that vices will exist, while men do. And so, while they study to anticipate human wickedness, and that by arts, which experience and long practice have taught, and which men generally use under the guidance more of fear than of reason, they are thought to be enemies of religion, especially by divines, who believe that supreme authorities should handle public affairs in accordance with the same rules of piety, as bind a private individual. Yet there can be no doubt, that statesmen have written about politics far more happily than philosophers. For, as they had experience for their mistress, they taught nothing that was inconsistent with practice.

"And, certainly, I am fully persuaded that experience has revealed all conceivable sorts of commonwealth, which are consistent with men's living in unity, and likewise the means by which the multitude may be guided or kept within fixed bounds. So that I do not believe that we can by meditation discover in this matter anything not yet tried and ascertained, which shall be consistent with experience or practice. For men are so situated, that they cannot live without some general law. But general laws and public affairs are ordained and managed by men of the utmost acuteness, or, if you like, of great cunning or craft. And so it is hardly credible, that we should be able to conceive of anything serviceable to a general society, that occasion or chance has not offered, or that men, intent upon their common affairs, and seeking their own safety, have not seen for themselves.

"Therefore, on applying my mind to politics, I have resolved to demonstrate by a certain and undoubted course of argument, or to deduce from the very condition of human nature, not what is new and unheard of, but only such things as agree best with practice. And that I might investigate the subject-matter of this science with the same freedom of spirit as we generally use in mathematics, I have laboured carefully, not to mock, lament, or execrate, but to understand human actions; and to this end I have looked upon passions, such as love, hatred, anger, envy, ambition, pity, and the other perturbations of the mind, not in the light of vices of human nature, but as properties, just as pertinent to it, as are heat, cold, storm, thunder, and the like to the nature of the atmosphere, which phenomena, though inconvenient, are yet necessary, and have fixed causes, by means of which we endeavor to understand their nature, and the mind has just as much pleasure in viewing them aright, as in knowing such things as flatter the senses.

"For this is certain, and we have proved its truth in our Ethics, that men are of necessity liable to passions, and so constituted as to pity those who are ill, and envy those who are well off; and to be prone to vengeance more than to mercy: and moreover, that every individual wishes the rest to live after his own mind, and to approve what he approves, and reject what he rejects. And so it comes to pass, that, as all are equally eager to be first, they fall to strife, and do their utmost mutually to oppress one another; and he who comes out conqueror is more proud of the harm he has done to the other, than of the good he has done to himself. And although all are persuaded, that religion, on the contrary, teaches every man to love his neighbor as himself, that is to defend another's right just as much as his own, yet we showed that this persuasion has too little power over the passions. It avails, indeed, in the hour of death, when disease has subdued the very passions, and man lies inert, or in temples, where men hold no traffic, but least of all, where it is most needed, in the law-court or the palace. We showed too, that reason can, indeed, do much to restrain and moderate the passions, but we saw at the same time, that the road, which reason herself points out, is very steep; so that such as persuade themselves, that the multitude of men distracted by politics can ever be induced to live according to the bare dictate of reason, must be dreaming of the poetic golden age, or of a stage-play."[23]

Spinoza is quite sober as to the social potentialities of altruism. But, as he emphasized in *The Ethics,* reason makes no demands which are contrary to man's nature. Indeed, "it demands that every man should love himself, should seek that which is useful to him."[24] To Spinoza, this "self-seeking" nature, which, we must emphasize again, is the opposite of self-indulgence, is the most valuable item in the composition of man; and he goes as far as to identify "self-seeking" with virtue. We all know that the denial of human instincts is bound to produce insoluble conflicts in man. Self-realization is the law of life, and so-called ideals which contradict this law will go the way of those who seek to conquer nature by breaking her laws, instead of obeying and thereby mastering them.

Spinoza, long before Freud, understood that repressed instinctual impulses must come to the person's awareness, so that they can be controlled and thus brought into harmony with the human personality and the society in

[23] *Ibid.,* Vol. I, pp. 287-289.
[24] *Ibid.,* Vol. II, p. 201.

which he lives. Though himself inclined to lead an almost ascetic life, he rejected self-renunciation as a false front, as an attempt to fool others, and oneself. He realized that the preacher who always thunders against the "flesh" is most likely the worst sinner, if not in deed, obviously in thought. In accordance with his upbringing in the Jodenburt, Spinoza insisted that man must achieve salvation in this world by mutual aid in associative life and not by an escape into a monastery or the world of the beyond. *Hic Rhodus, hic salta!* Let the theologians decry "sin" and glory in their own "righteousness"; let Hobbes admire brutality; let Rousseau who lived so complacently on the bounty of his mistresses and sent his children to the foundling asylum, let him demand the return to "nature"; men, Spinoza knew, will find out some day that only by cooperation, by enlightened self-interest can they avoid the dangers that lurk in their own ambivalence.

Fear of solitude and the realization of the usefulness of social organization are prime causes of societal growth. Man does not join society because he has ready-made social instincts. He develops his social mindedness as a result of joining human organizations, "for men are not born fit for citizenship, but must be made so."[25] And only as their intelligence increases in their relationship with other human beings, do men participate in making this world a better planet for their existence.

"The formation of society serves not only for defensive purposes, but is also very useful, and, indeed, absolutely necessary, as rendering possible the division of labour. If men did not render mutual assistance to each other, no one would have either the skill or the time to provide for his own sustenance and preservation: for all men are not equally apt for all work, and no one would be capable

[25] *Ibid.*, Vol. I, p. 313.

of preparing all that he individually stood in need of. Strength and time, I repeat, would fail, if every one had in person to plough, to sow, to reap, to grind, to cook, to weave, to stitch, and perform the other numerous functions required to keep life going; to say nothing of the arts and sciences which are also entirely necessary to the perfection and blessedness of human nature. We see that peoples living in uncivilized barbarism lead a wretched and almost animal life, and even they would not be able to acquire their few rude necessaries without assisting one another to a certain extent."[26]

If men were by nature "social," society would have no need for laws. There is no sober man who would not wish to live in serenity. Or as the "Beggar's Opera" says, "Wermöchte nicht in Fried und Eintracht leben, doch die Verhältnisse, sie sind nicht so."

Indeed, if men lived under the guidance of their enlightened self-interest, "everyone would remain in possession of this his right, without any injury being done to his neighbour (IV. xxxv. Coroll. i.). But seeing that they are a prey to their emotions, which far surpass human power or virtue (VI. vi.), they are often drawn in different directions, and being at variance one with another (IV. xxxiii. xxxiv.), stand in need of mutual help (IV. xxxv. note). Wherefore, in order that men may live together in harmony, and may aid one another, it is necessary that they should forego their natural right, and, for the sake of security, refrain from all actions which can injure their fellow-men. The way in which this end can be attained, so that men who are necessarily a prey to their emotions (IV. iv. Coroll.), inconstant, and diverse, should be able to render each other mutually secure, and feel mutual trust, is evident from IV. vii, and III. xxxix. It is there shown,

[26] *Ibid.*, Vol. I, p. 73.

that an emotion can only be restrained by an emotion stronger than, and contrary to itself, and that men avoid inflicting injury through fear of incurring a greater injury themselves."[27]

How to frame the laws so that the greatest possible number of men and women may find their own security and chance for self-development under their protection —this is the problem for the trained politician. Spinoza knew that force is the essence of law; that law without law enforcement is a farce. "A commonwealth can only exist by the laws being binding on all. If all the members of a state wish to disregard the law, by that very fact they dissolve the state and destroy the commonwealth. Thus, the only reward which could be promised to the Hebrews for continued obedience to the law was security and its attendant advantages, while no surer punishment could be threatened for disobedience, than the ruin of the state and the evils which generally follow therefrom, in addition to such further consequences as might accrue to the Jews in particular from the ruin of their especial state."[28]

Like most philosophers, Spinoza loves order. But it is no artificial order which he wants, no Platonic Republic, no universal empire in the style of Dante, no Utopia à la More.

In Spinoza's view, whatever is conducive to human growth, to the maturing of man and man's fellowship, is "good"; and whatever hinders man's growth and makes for discord and destructiveness in society is "evil."

He recognized that all human development implies

[27] *Ibid.*, Vol. II, pp. 213-214.
[28] *Ibid.*, Vol. I, p. 47. Parenthetically, international law will not be binding law until the nations of the world create the necessary instruments of compulsion. If we are to prevent further wars, we must see to it that no nation may re-arm for aggression with impunity or attack a divided world with chances of success.

variation; and that variation may be taken as discord by those who cannot distinguish between construction and destruction. The social sanction of liberty lies in the potential value of variations. The essence of democracy is that it sanctions the right of individuals to differ from one another, the right of groups to cultural pluralism. To Spinoza the *raison d'être* of the state is to enable man to live out his life in freedom without trespassing on the freedom of his fellow man. Therefore, his advocacy of a citizen army with every citizen entitled to have arms at home. (*Political Treatise,* Chap. VII) Therefore, his plea against governmental centralism and his insistence on municipal pride, home rule, and local government responsibility. Therefore, his contention in all his writings that the insecurity of freedom is always preferable to the security of bondage.

But what if men failed to follow the laws of reason which make for the stability and survival of the commonwealth? What if they created dictatorships for the enslavement of the people, for the liquidation of "Jews and Marxists" in a Hitler Germany, of "Trotskyites and Cosmopolitans" in a Soviet Union? Spinoza did not advocate revolution or, like Locke, try to furnish the ethical justification for it. Instead he writes: "He that knows himself to be upright does not fear the death of a criminal, and shrinks from no punishment; his mind is not wrung with remorse for any disgraceful deed: he holds that death in a good cause is no punishment, but an honour, and that death for freedom is glory."[29]

The dictator will, in the end, be the author of his own downfall, just as the man who swallows poison, wittingly or unwittingly, is the author of his own fate. There will be revolution as the inevitable consequence—as inevitable

[29] *Ibid.,* Vol. I, p. 263.

as any natural phenomenon. No matter how long the dictatorship may last, in the end it is bound to crash. Spinoza who had made his peace with nature's laws also accepted without complaint the limitations of human life. His political philosophy was simply the logical extension of his concept of God. If everything in the universe was but a form or manifestation of an all-creative, all-pervading power which we are used to call God, the state, too, was but a natural phenomenon. It was the natural product of human nature, acting in response to the qualities of self-preservation and self-realization, qualities or laws which express the infinite power, God, of which they form an integral part.

Like any scientist worthy of the name, Spinoza did not try to discover things as they should be, had he been the creator, but as they are and why they are so. He did not deal with wishes or day dreaming. In Utopia or Augustine's City of God, there may be no need for the stark realism and honest evaluations which Spinoza displayed. There, away from the earth that we know, men and women may be purged of egoism. But here on earth, like it or not, human behavior is self-seeking; and to educate men to be social, to be altruistic, one will do well to remember human nature and create the conditions under which it can yield to altruism. This is the focal point in Spinoza's concept of the state. Let it be repeated, man is a political animal only in the sense that he finds political existence more useful to his concern with his self-preservation than a lonely, non-political existence. He creates the state, an Athenian city-state, a British empire, or a democratic republic like the United States of America because it satisfies basic urges of his nature. Had man the power (which he does not have) to secure self-preservation as an individual, he would not submit to the authority of the common or general will.

Confronted with the choice of non-submission and destructive anarchy or submission to authority and greater self-realization, he chooses human fellowship. Thus far, Spinoza is in accord with Machiavelli and Hobbes. But Spinoza, student of the Talmud and of Maimonides, was a more penetrating philosopher than the authors of *The Prince* and *Leviathan*. Might makes right. But what kind of might makes what kind of right? There is unintelligent and intelligent might, there is destructive and constructive might, there is despotic and democratic might. There is also despotic and communal right, inequitable and equitable right. Both sets of "might" and "right" will ultimately be tested by their utility for man. That system of might, or government, will and must emerge victorious which develops human nature so far as it can be liberated with safety for all. Spinoza was confident that, after trial and error, man will build his commonwealth on the basis of his social intelligence.

But how is this intelligence to spread before man's emotional make-up coupled with the deadly weapons forged by his technical know-how get the better or rather the worse of him and lead him into an all-out war of all-out destruction? It is at this point that the political philosophy of Spinoza betrays its weakest side. For seeing things *sub specie eternitatis,* he refuses to enter into detailed problems. We are, therefore, forced to seek the practical implications of his analysis ourselves by following the clues which he has given.

This much can be stated with certainty. With his ideas of popular sovereignty, of the common or general will, and of democracy in the modern sense Spinoza had paved the way for the French Declaration of Human Rights and the

American revolution. While no cult of political pragmatism bears his name, his utilitarian concept of the state, propagandized by Locke, Bentham, and Jefferson, forms the political basis of life in the Western world. He could not anticipate in concrete terms the challenge presented by Stalinist Russia to the social, cultural, and ethical values of our civilization. But the task of organizing the struggle against the Communist version of the Hegelian "Law of Strife" is made easier by the fact that Spinoza did some extraordinary, profound thinking in the seventeenth century. For it should be remembered that the power of good logic broke the chains which the medieval method of thought had clamped on the human mind; and it cannot be assumed that the force of logical arguments has been diminished in the 300 years since Spinoza.

It is no accident that in countries which cherish the principles of individual liberty and responsibility, which allow freedom of thought, of speech, and of worship, which do not deprive their citizens of all incentive to use their intelligence and their ingenuity—that in these countries the material standard of living is much higher than in the orbit of the dictatorial Soviet Union. It is no accident either that, throughout history and in our own time, regimes which thwarted the creative initiative of their citizens have invariably collapsed. Athens perished after it had forced Socrates to drink the cup of hemlock. Spain, once the ruler of Europe and a large part of America, after the persecution of the Jews, Spinoza's ancestors among them, declined into political insignificance. Hitler Germany, that was to last a thousand years, lasted from 1933 to 1945.

This, then, appears to be a law of history, that a society which shuts out its most imaginative and creative thinkers, which demands conformity and orthodoxy, however mighty it may seem to be temporarily, will in the end be doomed to the very mediocrity which it tries to enforce among its members. For those who do not approve of conformity and police state methods, this law of history is a consolation in dark times.

Spinoza's Legacy for the Twentieth Century

SPINOZA PROPOSED no isms and no specific program for action. But he kindled a light in a dark street and opened the door to some of the most significant vistas in political science. While he taught us that the state is not the result of a deliberate social contract but rather the expression of a dynamic process of man's adaptation to his physical and mental environment, he established the fundamental conception that man, in the end, is responsible for his social institutions and that in many respects he makes his own destiny. For he observed that the evolutionary process can be accelerated by human intelligence; and he immunized us as best he could against irrational and demagogical appeals. Not content with a mere description of political phenomena or with an uncritical rehash of thin-worn rationalizations, he analyzed the human personality and the relevant data of human history in order to project the possibilities of man for the future.

Like many modern psychologists, foremost among them Sigmund Freud, Spinoza warned us to beware of wishful thinking and to reckon with established facts. But he also made it clear that this does not imply any fatalistic passivity; that to find life worthwhile, we must use our God-given creativeness to achieve "the good life" or, as some may call it, "the kingdom of God" on earth. Atheism, Spinoza taught us, is not the refusal to go to church every Sunday morning or to mumble formal prayers that may have lost their meaning and, therefore, their healing force, for the worshipper. Atheism is rather the despair of the reality of God; it is cynicism; it is to have lost faith in the struggle for a better, for a "messianic" future of the human race.

It seems obvious that we cannot fly a magic carpet, or change the course of the moon, and, except in fairy tales, we might as well forget to build castles in the sky. But we can build airplanes to allow human beings—and not only the wealthy among them—to visit foreign countries and get to know the mores of people everywhere. We can build esthetic and sanitary homes for virtually every family on earth. This and more lies within our power.

This, then, is the question: What could our universities, and what could our churches do for education, for enlightenment, for the organization and spreading of intelligence? They have influence, facilities, men and women who profess to be dedicated to the service of their fellowmen. What better way is there to make men love their neighbors than to make them understand one another? How better can religion combat "evil"? There is still truth in the world that "hungers to be felt or seen." There are still people in the world, the overwhelming majority of the human race, who do not obtain their "daily bread," who are undernourished, exploited, and oppressed. There are communists about who preach social justice but defend a system of government which calls Soviet millionaires and bureaucratic parasites "true proletarians" and subjects the masses of its citizens to poverty, genocide, and the pestilent atmosphere of insidious and ubiquitous terror. There are capitalists about who, while loudest in their opposition to all collectivist and socialist ideas, try every trick under the sun to eliminate their rivals from competition, making a mockery of the economic system of "free enterprise" which they profess to serve and to maintain. There is a growing number of men and women who believe that the world has become too big for them; who, confronted with science that, once hailed as a savior, has now forged the weapons of global destruction, are either paralyzed or panicky.

Is not perhaps the task of the men of religion and of the colleges once more to come forward with a concept of ethics that will keep our civilization alive and hopeful? Let us try to apply what we have learned from Baruch Spinoza to our age and to its particular needs. Let us start with the beginning.

Spinoza has taught us that there is no impulse in man that cannot be made useful in the ethical development of civilized life. We may call pugnacity and lust "bad" or "evil." But Spinoza emphasizes that these "vices" are but the perversions of human instincts which in themselves are nature-given, valuable and sound. Pugnacity is the perversion of self-display. There is obviously no "evil" in the boys who box honestly and with fairness in the boxing ring. But pugnacity which leads to the murder of another human being or to aggressive warfare is rightly considered "evil" by our society. Lust is the perversion of the sex instinct, which, directed to normal and right ends, makes for the stability of family ties and of wholesome social life. "Evil" then is the use of an impulse in the wrong place at the wrong time and toward the wrong objective. In a sense, it is perverted virtue.

There was a time when slavery was considered socially acceptable or "good", since it marked a decided step in advance of the earlier custom of killing off those who were captured in war. As we have progressed and matured, slavery, the "good" of yesterday, has become the "evil" of today. In fact, we cannot conceive of human progress without accepting at the same time the idea of "evil" as a sort of misplacement, or obsoleteness. For progress implies that we move on from what has been found "bad" or "evil" or unsatisfactory to something which we consider better and more satisfactory.

Our human aim has always been to build a complete human personality and a healthy society, mindful of the essential unity and rationality of the cosmos. This is what the religionist really means when he speaks of the Kingdom of Heaven. The urge to completeness is the most compelling urge of life. If a wound is inflicted on our body, every part of the bodily organism goes to work to restore and to heal the injured part. What happens to us physiologically, also happens to us mentally. If we felt no sense of incompleteness, there would be no need and no love of God. Why does the Bedouin gladly risk his life in a Yihad or Holy War? Because the promise of an oasis in heaven with lush gardens, fresh waters, and dark-eyed maidens describes exactly what he misses in the burning heat of the Arabian desert. What is man's dream of heaven, if not his hope to attain in heaven what he lacks on earth.

We know from our personal experiences that completeness of personality can never be gained by day dreams and phantasies. A man who, resentful of his inadequacy, imagines himself as a great prize fighter, does not simply become a prize fighter because of his phantasy. Phantasy is always extravagant. There is nothing wrong in seeking to do outstanding and significant things as long as they are not done at the expense of other human beings and as long as we do not flatter our vanity by thinking that we ought to conquer the sun. For then we might easily suffer the fate of Icarus. The completeness of our personality can only be produced by the harmonious expression of all our vital forces towards a common end. This thought, in different words, has been defined as the will toward self-realization.

Ordinarily, will cannot be moved by an ideal which is alien to the whole character of the person involved. An honest man will not steal, whatever the temptation. A man without integrity will gladly take "souvenirs." If he happens to be a member of the armed forces in a conquered nation, he will "liberate" Leicas, chinaware, and other valuables. If the members of his family at home have no more integrity than he possesses, they will receive the "liberated" items without scruples and even show them around to their friends, participating thereby in the demoralization of the society to which they belong.

But, as we also know, there are times when the sober man gets drunk and the kindly person brutal. Spinoza, to whom nothing human was foreign, showed us that this happens because the human personality can be stimulated by "adequate" as well as by "inadequate" ideals. There are men who put all their energy and all their intelligence into destructiveness, whether it is the violation of the liquor laws in the dormitory of a college campus, the organization of political subversion, or a bank theft. The morphine addict is often called a person of weak will. Actually, he should be called a person of misdirected will; for to secure a few grains of morphium he will move heaven and earth and demonstrate a dogged determination which is worthy of the finest causes.

What the "adequate" ideal is has never been clearly determined. It is the search of the artist, the philosopher, the man of religion, and the social scientist. The artist may call it beauty, the philosopher truth, the religious man

God, and the social scientist the good life. No one ideal has ever been universally accepted, and as Spinoza emphasized, we are apt to make errors in judgment. Should, then, every man be encouraged to pursue the path which seems to him to lead to his own Shangri-la and to blunder through life only to find at the end that he wasted his time?

There is the libertine who tells us that our instincts were given us to use and not to repress. But if this principle holds good, a soldier who runs away after hearing the first burst of a gunshell, instead of being court-martialed, ought to be congratulated for obeying his fear instinct. The thief caught red-handed in the jewelry shop should be praised for exercising his instinct of acquisition. What a world this would be!

It is the experience of the human race in all its segments and throughout the ages that libertinism is socially undesirable because it destroys associative life. But why not defy society? Why should we be bound by moral scruples and by the opinions of others? If we accept morality as an imposition from without, something unrelated to the laws of nature, there may be justification for such defiance. But the ten commandments, strangely enough, appear to be demands of our own biological and psychic makeup. Why should we try to keep alive the aged and the sick? Why should we not drown our helpless offspring, instead of nursing them until they become debutantes or college athletes? The answer is that there is such a thing as the maternal instinct, that there is a law of life necessary for the survival not only of the fittest but of the human species as such. Why should we not advocate "free love" and sexual promiscuity? Why is there a seventh commandment that admonishes us not to commit adultery? Societies which have tried "free love" either quickly returned to the family convention or disintegrated because they defied the biological goal of human nature, the reproduction of the race. The higher in evolution we go, the more emphasis we find on monogamy and on the development of family life which is to secure first of all the necessary protection for the mother during her reproductive period.

In the individual, sexual development follows that of the race. The boy of sixteen may flirt with several girls at once. However, having chosen the "right" partner, the monogamous impulse eventually emerges and seeks expression in marriage and the establishment of a family. The grown man who continues to express the polygamous impulses which were appropriate in his adolescence is recognized by women of sense not as a dashing hero but as a case of arrested development, as someone who instead of living according to nature has failed to keep in step with natural growth. The more we look about and into us, the more we realize that natural law and moral law are but two aspects of man's march toward self-realization. Moral laws, far from being opposed to the laws of nature, are the enunciation of the higher laws of biology.

As we have said before, there is no instinct in man that has not been of significance in the biological evolution of the race and could not be of value in its ethical growth. Those who urge us to repress our instincts before they get out of control, are, therefore, as ill-advised as the libertines who urge us not to restrain them. For they fail to realize that one cannot control what one represses. "Peace of soul" cannot be secured by rejecting and repressing passions which are unruly. It can be secured only to the extent to which we recognize our instincts and direct them toward individually and socially acceptable ends. Let us illustrate this point. If someone carelessly steps on my feet, it is quite natural for me to be angry. But it would serve no good purpose if I lost my temper and started a fist fight. If I repressed my anger and tried to pretend that it was just impossible for me ever to get angry, that I am by far too gentle to be emotionally aroused, more likely than not, my repressed temper would later come out toward my wife at home or my students in class on the most trifling pretext. We need not, we must not repress our impulses. Instead we must bring them into consciousness and under rational control.

The only but all-important criterion of self-realization is that it alone produces harmony and serenity in us, while acting according to impulse leaves us invariably shallow and deeply unsatisfied. For when we act according to impulse, when we follow the "pleasure principle", we obviously have no control over ourselves. We are victims of our passions; we are not free. St. Augustine, who knew from his own youth what a life of superficial pleasures meant, was, therefore, right in his paradox that we are only truly free to the extent to which we choose the good, to the extent to which we choose what makes for the completeness of our personality. We discover the "adequate" ideal, then, by the effect which our ideal has on us, by the serenity which it engenders.

No ideal affords harmony and serenity to the individual, unless it commends itself ultimately to the community. For no human being, gifted as he is with social potentials by his very nature, can forever be happy in complete isolation from his fellow men. Hillel, therefore, once remarked: "The uncultured man cannot be a saint." It was not "Pharisaic self-righteousness" which prompted him to use these words, echoed by Spinoza many centuries later. It was rather the recognition that every individual needs the stimulation of a group culture to grow and to mature. What is the foundation of religion? Is it faith or works, one's solitary reflections or one's social behavior? Actually, this bone of contention in "organized" religion poses an artificial dichotomy. Just as the group cannot exist without individuals nor the individual without some human association, religious life does not lie at one pole or another but rather it harmonizes solitariness and interrelatedness. We are interrelated with our fellow men in our daily needs. The prehistoric savage tried to "go it alone". Like his not too remote relations, the beasts of prey, he sneered at mutual aid and cooperation. He fought the elements without being able to harness them for his use; and when he died he left no memories behind him of his struggle beyond the crudest of tools. As man became more civilized, more conscious of his existence, he learned the meaning of "choice" and partnership. He began to practice a division of labor. He learned that no individual could thrive without contributing from his personal acquisitions toward the common welfare; that predatory groups like predatory individuals, perish from the earth, leaving but resentment behind them. Life, running its seemingly futile course, gained a sense of history only when a great lawgiver arose among the ancient Hebrews, bade them rebel against the ingrained habits of the human species throughout the past, and asked them to give dignity to their lives. Then, conscience came into the world. Then, man also began to understand that with all his creative intelligence, assisting him in increasing steadily his material comforts, he still was but a part of an interrelated universe and that he had to rely on the Creator for his salvation. Without faith, the physician, however little he may believe in formal, "organized" religion, would have no strength to devote a whole life and every ounce of energy to the cure of cancer or some other illness. Without faith, man is like a straw in the wind, like a ship without an anchor. In the last analysis, it is faith in an ordered, and, therefore, moral, universe, that makes our life meaningful and that allows us to conceive of our earthly existence as but a phase of life eternal.

Since the days of Moses' Sermon on Mount Sinai, God, translated into human terms, has always meant the enhancement of human life.[1] To enhance his life, man must learn to live in mutual aid, in a peaceful, lawful society with his fellow man. This implies the protection of the right of every man "to dwell safely under his vine and fig tree," an acute awareness of the interdependence of all the citizens of the state and of all nations. This implies the recognition of the brotherhood of all men, whatever their social status, their language, their nationality, their color, their race, their creed. This implies the gradual realization of Isaiah's vision:

"And they shall beat their swords into plowshares
And their spears into pruning hooks;
Nation shall not lift up sword against nation,
Neither shall they learn war any more."

Obviously there is no glib solution in the realization of this hope. Where the League of Nations failed, the United Nations Organization may fail too. Man's forward march is slow and slippery. But this must not weaken our determination to achieve a world in which all national groups, all civilizations will live under international law and abide by it. For we may have well reached the point at which man will either abolish war or be relegated to the jungle from which he freed himself by the use of his reason in thousands of years of civilizatory effort.

We in the Western world, in the footsteps of Spinoza, Locke, Montesquieu, and Jefferson have become accus-

[1] "If you choose good, you choose life. But if you choose evil, you choose death." (Deuteronomy 30:15).

tomed to demanding freedom of criticism and democratic government. Government, we must remember, is the name for the organization and the methods which human associations use in carrying out their functions. In a state with democratic government, the source of authority lies in the governed, in all the citizens who, therefore, reserve for themselves the means of bringing their representatives or government officials to account. In other words, the essentials of the democratic state are equality and liberty. While we may consider no theory of the state as ultimate truth, while because of longer experience we may be more sober in our belief as to a worldwide acceptance of democracy than the thinkers of the eighteenth and nineteenth centuries, we still assume with Spinoza that democratic government which carefully protects the right of free criticism is the most desirable form of government devised by human beings so far.

This concept of government is challenged in our day by communism with its center in the Soviet Union. During the second half of the nineteenth century, communism as it was called by some, socialism by others, demanded the end of the economic exploitation of the working classes, who in the decades immediately following the industrial revolution in England were indeed exploited and abused. It led to the organization of trade unions, the formation of the British Labor Party and a number of Social Democratic parties on the European continent and in the Americas. In their struggle against social inequality and unjust lordship over human life, they were thoroughly in tune with the democratic concept of government. It was only when Marx and, after him, Lenin, postulated the idea of the "dictatorship of the proletariat" and demanded a society in which all means of production are owned by the state, that the originally equalitarian and reformist movement lost its democratic motivation and, first in Russia, and now on Chinese soil, assumed the ugly despotic features which characterize political communism in the practices of our time. While Marx, under the influence of men like Robert Owen and Charles Fourier, still hoped that the social and economic equality of which he wrote in the *Communist Manifesto* would eventually change the very functions of government and render most of the state machinery superfluous, while Lenin echoed this idea in predicting that the state would "wither away," "Stalinism" has produced the very opposite, the police state, the totalitarian state.

Civilization is the endeavor to reduce violence to the *ultima ratio*. Lenin proclaimed violence as the *prima ratio*. His successors, foremost among them Stalin, made it the *unica ratio*. Once the barbarous element of violence, which true social reformers will always try to keep under lock and key, had won the day, indifference to truth and to ethical conceptions of equity led not only to the most ruthless one-party rule but even to the destruction of the less brutalized members of the Bolshevist "élite" itself. Political democracy and social democracy supplement each other. But there is no bridge between democracy, based on human enhancement, and Stalinist communism, based on human enslavement. This, of course, is not to mean the impossibility of bonds of friendship between the peoples of the West and the peoples of the Soviet orbit. To the contrary, in our physically interdependent world, we who enjoy the blessings bestowed upon us by what appears to be an "adequate" ideal, can not with impunity write off millions of human beings who have come under the sway of totalitarian tyranny. But we shall not be able to contain communism and to liberate its victims, unless we understand the mental climate in which communism flourishes.

In this respect, it should be remembered that it was the autocracy of Czarist Russia which bred that peculiar brand of Russian "professional revolutionaries" who, in 1903 at the convention of the Social Democratic Party in London, joined Lenin and broke away from the main stream of European democracy. Constantly under the shadow of arrest by the Czarist political police when they were in Russia, forced to live in poverty when they went abroad, these men and women developed all the characteristics of persecuted religious fanatics. Believing that they constituted an élite of humanity, they found a subconscious compensation for the frustrations of their daily lives in the gospel of revolutionary violence. Such an "élite", whether it bears the name of Bolshevists, Fascists, or Nazis, having but contempt for free discussion and majority decisions, can come to power only by force, by *coup d'état*. Trying to overcompensate for their social inferiority in the past, craving for approbation, the members of the "élite," once they achieve positions of power, feel compelled to sing their own praise at every street corner and to abuse their power. This is the story of the "Duce," the "Fuehrer," the "heroic father of his peoples," and their immediate followers.

If it wants to retain its power, the "élite" must be willing to apply force ruthlessly and instantaneously. If it weakens, if its members show signs of humanitarian scruples, it opens the way for a democratic revolution or promotes the rise of a new ruling minority of more unscrupulous careerists. This, again, is the reason for the perennial purges and liquidations within the ranks of the ruling cliques in all totalitarian systems of government.

For a while, riding on the crest of the democratic wave of 1917, the Leninist "élite" made its concessions to the equalitarian forces among the Russian masses, to their desire to do away with masters and servants, rich and poor. As long as Trotsky led the Red Army, officers and men wore the same kind of uniform and ate the same kind of food in the same canteens. There was no saluting, there were no insignia, no epaulettes. By the decree of November 18, 1919, all insurance for life, capital, and income was abolished; and no member of the communist party or the Soviet bureaucracy was to receive a higher salary than a qualified industrial worker. For a brief period, dreams of social justice seemed to cease to be mere abstractions. But Lenin and Trotsky had come to power by the betrayal of the Russian democratic revolution, by imprisoning, on January 20, 1918, the majority of the deputies of Russia's first and only genuine parliamentary representation, the Constituent Assembly, by taking the land from the peasants instead of giving them land as they had promised, by reviving Ivan the Terrible's Oprichina under the name of Cheka. Bolshevism, from its very beginning, has fought against the sanctity of the home, the moral equality of every human being, and simple human kindness. It has forced an unfortunate Russian nation into a colossal pathological adventure from which there can be no return to normal life as long as there is a Bolshevist party in Russia based on terroristic minority rule.

Once most of the "Old Bolshevists," among them Trotsky, Bucharin, Kamenev, and Zinoviev were "liquidated," there was not even any further need for paying lip service to the equalitarian ideas which had been the cause, or at least the rationalization, of Lenin's associates in their struggle for political power. The "New Bolshevists," those who form the top layer of the Soviet bureaucracy since the purges of 1936-37, revived the institution of inherited privilege, abolished free education in institutions of higher learning, introduced "Stakhanovism" even in the concentration camps, reintroduced rank and subordination in the armed forces, and burned the history books written during the Leninist period. Theirs appears to be a technological outlook on life, delighting in the fireworks of production statistics and in the promise that the human automaton deliberately fashioned in Soviet society is destined to conquer the earth.

For the Western world to appease such a system of government would be to encourage its aggressiveness and to strengthen its hold on the peoples of the Soviet orbit. Ours, in a sense, is the task of the psychotherapist who assists his patient in wresting his suppressed instincts from their morbid attachments and in harnessing them to the use of a more harmonious personality. Appeasement of aggression is poor psychotherapy. In the end, it destroys both the doctor and the patient. Aggression, as Spinoza knew so well, must be met by firm resistance, a just estimate of its character, and a wise dealing with it. It must never be forgotten that our aim is to bring about peaceful, neighborly governments in Russia and in China and not the destruction or degradation of Russia or China as nations. Containment of Soviet aggression must therefore be combined with the liberation of its victims into a grand therapeutic system which allows the masses of Russia and China to share in the healing process.

Hitlerism, insisting with Pareto, Sorel, and others, that the real determinations of the state are never shaped by the common will of the people and proclaiming the political superiority of the "Aryan" race, was in a sense a nationalistic disease that affected and still affects in various forms much of humanity. In a similar way, Stalinism, a diabolic perversion of man's craving for social security, is a disease which afflicts us all; and to the extent to which we blind ourselves to the needs of the underprivileged of this world, we share collective responsibility.

At the same time, we must remember that the international community is a group of legally independent states which tolerate no intervention. Whether we accept their sovereignty only as a concept of constitutional law or whether we adhere to the pluralist view which challenges the whole idea of the sovereign state, the fact, observed by Spinoza in his *Political Treatise* remains that "if one commonwealth wishes to make war on another and employ extreme measures to make that other dependent on itself, it may lawfully make the attempt, since it needs but the bare will of the commonwealth for war to be waged. But concerning peace it can decide nothing, save with the concurrence of another commonwealth's will. Whence it follows, that laws of war regard every commonwealth by itself, but laws of peace regard not one, but at the least two commonwealths, which are therefore called 'contracting powers'."[2]

We in the West, particularly in the United States of America, are today prone to complain about the "bad faith" which Stalin and his successors have demonstrated in their dealings with the Western nations after the end of the Second World War. But who gave lend-lease to a Soviet government which had signed the Molotov-Ribbentrop Pact of August 1939, which had opened no "second front" when France was invaded by the Nazis in the summer of 1940 and when the European democracies were on the verge of defeat? Who welcomed the Soviet government into the United Nations after the kidnapping of the Polish underground leaders invited by the Soviet government to come to Moscow for the discussion of the establishment of a Polish provisional government in pur-

[2] *Ibid.*, Vol. I, p. 307.

suance of the Yalta agreement? Who encouraged the communist drive into the heart of China by agreeing to the Soviet Russian annexation of the southern part of Sakhalin, the Soviet Russian occupation of the Manchurian port of Dairen, and the Soviet administration of both the Chinese Eastern Railroad and the South Manchurian Railroad? Who, finally, let the communist rulers in Moscow and Peking know that the United States would not defend Indo-China against the communist Viet Minh?

Listen to Spinoza. "If then a commonwealth complains that it has been deceived, it cannot properly blame the bad faith of another contracting commonwealth, but only its own folly in having entrusted its own welfare to another party that was independent."[3] Today, as three hundred years ago when Spinoza wrote the *Political Treatise*, it must be assumed that a state may do most anything in the realm of foreign policy that it has the power to do. To this day, no state can be compelled to submit its disputes with another state to the rulings of an international court judging under international law. It may be well to argue that, as the liberty of the individual is not absolute, as his freedom is subject to limitations in the interests of the local or national community, so the independence of the individual states ought to be restricted in the interests of the international community. While international law, based on international ethical principles, has had some influence on international relations, these relations are still conducted, as in Spinoza's days, in an atmosphere in which everybody carries a gun.

Woodrow Wilson was too optimistic when he told the Congress of the United States in 1917: "We are at the beginning of an age in which it will be insisted that the same standards of conduct and of responsibility for wrong

[3] *Ibid.*, Vol. I, p. 307.

shall be observed among nations and their governments that are observed among the individual citizens of civilized states." Today, almost half a century after these words of a great American president were spoken, we are still "at the beginning." If we ask for the reason, an honest answer will not only review the social heterogeneity of the states in the world community, with their differences in educational and economic standards, religious toleration and political maturity. It will also emphasize that, notwithstanding the Inter-American Defense Treaty and NATO, the Western nations themselves, in spite of their common background and aspirations, have not yet been willing to overcome their parochial egoisms, pool their resources, and create a nucleus of world government which would be strong enough to secure liberty and peace. It will, finally, include the sober fact that we, the citizens of the United States, Wilson's country, have not yet fully accepted the idea that international law is not a one way street and that we, too, must submit to it.

Yet, ultimately, we here must prove to the rest of the world that government by consent is superior to government by force; that democracy while granting equality of educational opportunity to all, values intellectual excellency, moral courage and scientific truth; that democracy makes for greater social justice than any totalitarian society; that democracy is better equipped to eliminate the demagogue than any other form of government; that democracy is able to translate man's yearning for peace into the reality of international life, and that it can release man from the scourge of war and the slavery of fear.

Spinoza, in all his writings, searched for a way of life which harmonizes the intelligence and activity of man with the nature of the universe under conditions of maximum freedom for the development of man's talents and abilities. To survive the totalitarian onslaught, democracy must never give up this search for man's salvation in this world.

INDEX

Acosta, Uriel, 7-9
Aquinas, Thomas, 3, 58
Aristotle, 3
Ashkenazim, 7
Atheism, 123
Augustine, 118, 129

Babylonian captivity, 74
Bacon, Francis, 15-6
Benedict XIII, 4
Bentham, Jeremy, 98, 120
Beth Jaakov, 10, 12
B'nai B'rith, 74
Brahman, 79
Bucharin, 135
Buddhism, 79
Burgh, Albert, 18

Cabbalah, 5
Calvinism, 9
Catholicism, also Catholic, 7, 13, 38
    Catholic Church, 75, 81-2, 89
Cheka, 135
Chosen people, 75
Christendom, also Christianity, 2, 13, 15, 28, 30
    Christian, 58, 75, 80-1, 87
Christ killer, 87
Church Council, Lateran, 4
Collegiants, 15
Communism, 56, 66, 109
    also Communist party, 120, 123
    Communist, 132-3
    (Bolshevist), 134-5
Cromwell, Oliver, 5

Dante, 116
Demagogue, 87
Descartes, 32, 38, 44
    also Cartesians, 45-6, 48, 50, 106
Deus sive natura, 40, 42, 47

DeVries, Simon, 19, 20, 27
De Witt, Jan, 20, 23

Einstein, Albert, 39, 78
Ezra, 70
Ezra, Abraham ibn, 3

Fascists, also fascist, 56, 109, 134
Fourier, Charles, 133
Freud, Sigmund, also Freudian, 14, 39, 46, 55, 113, 122

Gabirol, Solomon ibn, 2
Galileo, 9, 106
Gandhi, 78
Gnosticism, 6
Goethe, 13, 39, 71
Grotius, 21, 90

Halevi, Jehuda, 3
Hegel, also Hegelian, 120
Heidelberg University, 21-2
Herem, 12
Herzl, Theodor, 34
Hillel, 8, 129
Hinduism, 79
Hitler, 37, 117
Hobbes, also Hobbesian, 46-7, 50, 55-6, 91-2, 94, 97, 105, 114, 119
Hume, David, 35

Immortality, 54, 72
International Law, 90, 116
Isaiah, 67, 131
Islam, 79, 82
Israel, Manassah ben, 5
Israel, state of, 8

Jefferson, 120, 131
Jesus of Nazareth, 2, 73-5, 80, 85-7
Johai, Simon ben, 6
Judaism, 8, 14-5, 39, 58, 70, 81-2, 85, 87

141

INDEX

Kamenev, 135
Kant, also Kantian, 36
Kerkering, 10
Kohn, Eugene, 66

Labor Party (British), 132
League of Nations, 131
Leibnitz, 16
Lenin, also Leninist, 37, 132-6
Libertinism, 127
Locke, John, also Lockeian, 35, 56, 90, 94, 97, 117, 120, 131
Louis XIV, 90
Lucas, Jean Maximilian, 14
Luther, Martin, 81

Maccabees, 2
Machiavelli, also Machiavellian, 101, 119
Madariaga, Salvador de, 5
Maimonides, 3, 58, 119
Mao Tse Tung, 37
Marranos, 4, 7
Marx, Karl, also Marxist, 91, 117, 132-3
Mendelssohn, Moses, 39
Meyer, Lodwijk, 20, 34
Mohammed, 75-6
Molotov-Ribbentrop Pact, 137
Montefiore, Claude, 87
Morteira, 5
Montesquieu, 131
Moral Laws, 128
Moreh Nebuchim, 3
Moses, 61, 75, 131

Natura naturans, 42
Natura naturata, 42
Niddui, 12
Nietzsche, 13, 92
NATO, 139
Notiones communes, 44

Oldenburg, Henry, 20, 25, 32, 84
Oprichina, 135
Owen, Robert, 133

Palestine, also Hebrew-Palestinian, 58, 80
Pantheism, 90
Pareto, 136

Pharisees, also Pharisaic, 8, 61, 86, 129
Philo, 3
Plato, also Platonic, 3, 16, 36, 38, 43, 116
Portugal, also Portuguese, 2, 4, 5, 7, 8
Protestant revolt, 81
Psychoanalysis, 14

Reubeni, David, 6
Rieuwertz, Johann, 14, 20, 34
Rousseau, 13, 55, 90, 114

Savonarola, 101
Scholasticism, 8
Seneca, 99
Sephardim, 4
Social Democracy, 132, 134
Socrates, also Socratic, 71, 120
Sorel, 136
Soviet Union, also Soviet government 66, 120, 132-3, 135-8
Spain, also Spanish, 2, 89, 90
Stakhanovism, 135
Stalin, also Stalinist, 120, 133, 136-7
Stoa, 80

Talmud, 3, 119
Testament, New, 26
Testament, Old, 9, 26, 33, 70, 75
Tractatus Brevis, 14
Trotsky, also Trotskyites, 117, 135
Turkey, 5
Tydemann, Daniel, 24

United Nations, 131, 137
Universal Faith, 83

Van den Ende, 9-11
Viet Minh, 138
Voltaire, 38

Wilson, Woodrow, 138-9
Wolf, Abraham, 14

Yad Hasakah, 3
Yihad, 125

Zevi, Sabbatai, 6
Zinoviev, 135
Zohar, 6